FUNCTIONAL TEACHING
OF THE
MENTALLY RETARDED

Second Edition

FUNCTIONAL TEACHING
OF THE
MENTALLY RETARDED

By

MAX G. FRANKEL, M.Ed., Ph.D.
Professor of Special Education and Individualized Services
Kean College of New Jersey
Union, New Jersey

F. WILLIAM HAPP, Ph.D.
Staff Consultant
Laradon Hall Training and Residential Center for the Mentally Retarded
Denver, Colorado

MAURICE P. SMITH, Ph.D.
Late Professor of Psychology
University of Colorado
Boulder, Colorado

With a Foreword by
Edgar A. Doll, Ph.D.
Late Consulting Psychologist
Bellingham Public Schools
Bellingham Washington

CHARLES C THOMAS · PUBLISHER
Springfield · Illinois · U.S.A.

Published and Distributed Throughout the World by
CHARLES C THOMAS • PUBLISHER
BANNERSTONE HOUSE
301-327 East Lawrence Avenue, Springfield, Illinois, U.S.A.

© *1966 and 1975, by* CHARLES C THOMAS • PUBLISHER
ISBN 0-398-03361-7
Library of Congress Catalog Card Number: 74 23457

First Printing, 1966
Second Printing, 1967
Third Printing, 1969
Fourth Printing, 1971
Second Edition, 1975

With THOMAS BOOKS *careful attention is given to all details of manufacturing and design. It is the Publisher's desire to present books that are satisfactory as to their physical qualities and artistic possibilities and appropriate for their particular use.* THOMAS BOOKS *will be true to those laws of quality that assure a good name and good will.*

Printed in the United States of America
N-1

Library of Congress Cataloging in Publication Data

Frankel, Max G
    Functional teaching of the mentally retarded.

    Bibliography: p.
    Includes indexes.
    1. Mentally handicapped children—Education.
I. Happ, F. William, joint author. II. Smith, Maurice P., joint author. III. Title [DNLM: 1. Education of mentally retarded. LC4601 F829f]
LC4601.F68 1975   371.9'28   74-23457
ISBN 0-398-03361-7

To

Joseph V. and Elizabeth Calabrese,
the Founders of Laradon Hall,
and their two sons
Larry and Donald

History of Science reveals to us two kinds of phenomena, opposite as it were: at times, simplicity is hidden behind apparent complexities; at other times, on the contrary, we find that behind apparent simplicity hide extremely complicated realities.

HENRI POINCARE
In Dantzig, Tobias.
Henri Poincaré: critic of crises

FOREWORD

Now and then in the course of a professional lifetime one encounters colleagues who are gifted with the imagination, resourcefulness and initiative that each of us so earnestly strives for himself. Such an experience is at hand for those students of special education, including parents, who believe that instruction for the severely retarded should not be merely more of the same for longer periods and under greater pressure. Rather, what is sorely needed is the development of devices which are capable of decontaminating a special child's previous frustrations by giving him the experience of success and a renewal of his original eagerness for learning.

Mr. McGlone is one of those educational leaders who demonstrates that the impossible is only so because the solutions are not immediately self-evident. By an empirical development of imagination he has used the salvage principle not only with his students but also with his materials and methods. Here is a philosophy, a method and materials of education which fire the imagination and structure the courage of the teacher as well as that of the pupil. Here is an exemplification of the principle that education science is uncommon use of the commonplace. The remarkable success of Mr. McGlone has been well systemized in a simply formulated theory and philosophy of learning by the authors of this volume. They have caught the gleam of Mr. McGlone's inspiration and have reflected it to the reader in terms which are readily comprehended. The simplest ideas are the most difficult to rationalize.

It was my good fortune to see Mr. McGlone at work in the early days of his endeavors. I natuarally wondered how much of his apparent skill might be the result of discovering hidden talents on the part of his students and how much of his success was due to his personal skills and how much to his methods as such. My evaluation confirmed the professional judgment of others that these pupils were really severely retarded in intelligence, in neuromuscular aptitudes and particularly in initiative or motivation. It is a special tribute to the techniques described in this book that they do so succesfully stimulate the handicapped child to the rebirth of enthusiasm, effort and achievement.

Those who read this book, or who see any of the five motion picture films which portray this content in audio-visual terms, will surely experience new hope for capitalizing the educational potentials of "the least of these."

EDGAR A. DOLL, PH.D.

PREFACE

IN 1959, LARADON HALL SCHOOL for Exceptional Children published *Helpful Hints for Handicaps* by Roy "Dolly" McGlone. This monograph presented a brief description of a number of exercises Mr. McGlone had worked out in his efforts to teach mentally retarded children. Most of the exercises were unusual and all had become a part of an ambitious teaching program which Mr. McGlone was developing. The exercises were devised to aid the improvement of motor coordination, manual dexterity, attention span, and reasoning ability. It was his feeling that while such development normally occurs on the basis of informal learning experiences, the retarded child must be aided by providing more specific, formal learning opportunities.

The efforts Mr. McGlone was making came to the attention of a number of educators, vocational rehabilitation workers, psychologists, occupational therapists and others who were interested in the problems of mentally retarded people. Visitors to Mr. McGlone's classes were struck by the imaginative approach to teaching which he had developed. The results of his teaching, although difficult to evaluate precisely, were encouraging. Hence, an attempt was made to study systematically his methods and to relate his approach to that of other teachers as well as to the theories of mental development. A brief review of the background of Mr. McGlone's work may be found in Rosenblum (36).

A grant (No. RD-730) from the vocational Rehabilitation Administration of the Department of Health, Education, and Welfare aided in the preparation of *A Guide for Functional Teaching of Mentally Retarded Children*. In addition, the University of Colorado and Laradon Hall School for Exceptional Children contributed materially to support the publication of the guide. That guide in a revised form has been incorporated into this book.

Laradon Hall School for Exceptional Children, within which

developed the teaching program described in this book, was founded in Denver, Colorado, in 1948 by Joseph and Elizabeth Calabrese. Enrollment (which includes both day or residential students) is limited to the mentally retarded, within the IQ range of 25 to 70. The staff, numbering about sixty, includes an educational and a vocational director, teachers, speech therapist, psychologists, consulting dentist, physicians and psychiatrist, nurses, recreation counsellors, social workers and other professional personnel. The physical plant consists of classrooms, dormitories, gymnasium, swimming pool, vocational workshops, play areas, etc. Most of the older students work as trainees at tasks on contract work obtained from various firms, for which they are paid as a part of this training (see Rosenblum, 36).

This book is intended to be a practical use to teachers as a textbook for use in teacher training institutions, and of general interest to school administrators, occupational therapists, speech therapists, physicians, rehabilitation workers, psychologists, social workers and others who work with the mentally retarded. Perhaps an important use will be as an aid to teachers of the "trainable" retarded. Many of the exercises and techniques were developed for mentally retarded children within the IQ range of 25 to 50. Some of the elementary exercises may be useful for more severely retarded children, and many of the exercises and techniques described here should be helpful for "educable" mentally retarded children (i.e., children with IQ's from 50 to 75).

Those individuals who have participated in the preparation of this book include Professor Minnie S. Behrens, Omer A. Dery, and Patricia A. Luger. Cecelia Cudmore and Shirley McAuliffe gave secretarial help. We wish to express our appreciation for the editorial work of Patricia O'Connor Schommer and the assistance of Robert Crosson.

We wish to acknowledge the valuable assistance of the following teachers of retarded children representing various geographic areas of the United States who offered comments and suggestions on the Part II portion: Phyllis Bailey, Dorothy M. Givan, Sister Mary Andrews, S.S.J., Marilyn Olson, and Leon Van Wynsberghe. It would be impossible to mention the many others whose efforts benefited this book.

We are grateful for the comments and constructive criticism made during various stages of preparation of this book by Michael J. Begab, Rudolph J. Capobianco, Edgar A. Doll, Arnold Fassler, Thomas E. Jordan, Newell C. Kephart, Wayne L. Sengstock and Wesley D. White.

Finally, we cannot overemphasize our appreciation to the teachers and staff members of Laradon Hall School for Exceptional Children for their gracious cooperation.

Each reader will vary in his purpose for reading this book. For those whose intention it is to become familiar with Functional Teaching as a total program the following suggestion is made. Read the first three chapters of Part I carefully, then page through Part II before continuing with the remaining chapters of Part I.

Max G. Frankel
F. William Happ
Maurice P. Smith

INTRODUCTION TO THE
SECOND EDITION

THIS SECOND EDITION retains almost all of the structure and content of the previous edition but for minor changes and contains additional updated material, including resource material for the practitioner, which will be found in the appendix and may be helpful in educational planning.

Perhaps most significant is the change in terminology which is consonant with trends in the field. The terms developmental disability, developmental, and perceptually handicapped are used interchangeably with the term mentally retarded. These terms are more generic and, in this context, more definitive and therefore more useful. It is also within the philosophy of this text which is to label the program rather than the child.

Acknowledgement is made to Sister Rose Mary Colavito, Zelda Tannenbaum, Samuel Steckel and our many students and colleagues for their helpful criticism and assistance.

The authors wish to express their appreciation to Grune and Stratton and Charles C Thomas, Publisher for permission to reproduce portions of materials used in this text.

Co-author Maurice P. Smith (1920-1971) and Roy "Dolly" McGlone (1886-1974), who originated the program, have passed on as has Edgar A. Doll (1889-1968) who wrote the Preface. These beloved colleagues represented lifetimes of dedication of a kind seldom seen, ones which provided inspiration to their students and fellow workers of a quality rarely felt. To their blessed memory this Second Edition is dedicated.

M.G.F.
F.W.H.

ACKNOWLEDGMENTS

FOR THEIR HELP and assistance with the photographs and illustrations, we wish to thank James B. Henderson of Thorne Films, Inc., Boulder, Colo.; John Spindler; R. D. Seible; University of Colorado; The Associated Press and Thomas Fast.

M.G.F.
F.W.H.
M.P.S.

CONTENTS

Contents   xix

PART II
AREAS OF INSTRUCTION

FUNCTIONAL TEACHING
OF THE
MENTALLY RETARDED

PART I

FUNCTIONAL TEACHING:
PRINCIPLES AND PRACTICES

Chapter 1

INTRODUCTION TO FUNCTIONAL TEACHING

T HE FUNCTIONAL TEACHING approach is based on the conviction that instruction must be sensitive to the behavioral deficiencies peculiar to the mentally retarded. It is not enough simply to slow down or "water down" a normal program. Rather, one must become aware of each child's deficiencies, and devise exercises that will correct, as much as possible, these deficiencies. The corrections made must be such that they will contribute to further development of the child, that is, they must have transfer value for other aspects of the child's life. The program to be discussed and described here has grown out of observation of the behavior of retarded children and out of systematic efforts to help the children correct their deficiencies.

THE NATURE OF FUNCTIONAL TEACHING

This approach makes no great assumptions regarding a child's available behaviors (readiness, for example). Rather, by analysis of complex activities into simple elements which can be combined or recombined in almost any manner, it is possible for the teacher to seek achievements not commonly regarded as feasible for trainable or educable retarded children.

The implications of such a philosophy of the education or training of retarded children are many. Among these is the likelihood that suitable objectives can be based only on an evaluation of the global inventory of available functions. We need to perfect procedures for identification of these potentials (see Chapter 3, pp. 24, 25).

The following may be posed as distinguishing characteristics of the functional program:

1. It deals with functions (rather than etiologies), actions, and performances.
2. It concentrates on abilities rather than on disabilities. It

5

concentrates on the realm of possibility, and encourages behaviors, however simple, that lie within the child's abilities to function within a given situation.

3. Its goal is to enable the child to function within a wide scope of personal, social, and vocational behaviors.

FUNCTIONAL TEACHING AS A PROGRAM

It would be unrealistic to aim for broad behavioral objectives when these are not based on specific objectives which, in turn, are determined by observable functions. A teacher who wishes to observe these functions will come to be acutely aware of the characteristics of retarded children. More will be said of these shortly.

There may be a tendency for teachers and others working with the retarded to regard many of the specific approaches and methods described here as suitable only for children of low IQ. However, it must be remembered that retarded children, regardless of their place in the range of intellect, may lack basic skills. The prospective user of the approaches and methods of functional teaching should also realize that the so-called basic skills can often be broken down into still more fundamental skills. If teaching techniques can be applied to these underlying skills then the unfortunate results of frustration and failure, often dismissed by the statement that the child is retarded, may be overcome or, in some instances, avoided.

CHARACTERISTICS OF DEVELOPMENTALLY DISABLED CHILDREN

Every individual is different from every other individual. This is a truism that is sometimes overlooked in teaching mentally retarded children. Many individual characteristics must be considered in developing a program of instruction for a child. The types of exercises described in this book have been used with educable and trainable retarded children who differ considerably from one another in the characteristics listed below. In the light of the individual characteristics of each child the teacher will find it necessary to vary some details of each exercise, such as length of time spent or degree of proficiency demanded.

The following, we believe, are the most important deficiencies commonly found in retarded children, to which a teacher must be particularly responsive. Children will differ in the presence or absence of these characteristics and in the degree to which they are involved.

Apathy.

Impulsiveness—lack of behavior control, hyperactivity.

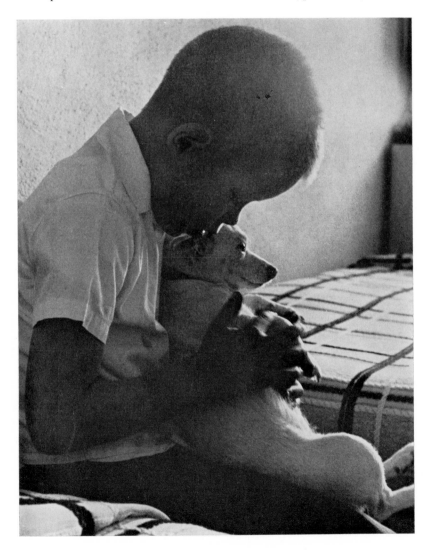

Emotional instability—irritability, fluctuation of mood.
Distractibility.
Low stamina—fatigued easily.
Motor disabilities—spasticity, palsy, crippling.
Over-dependence upon others.
Lack of curiosity.
Sensory impairment—defective sight, hearing, etc.
Disorders of perception—short attention span, figure-ground confusion, attention to irrelevant features.
Disorders in concept formation—lowered reasoning ability.
Language disorders—speech difficulties, extremely limited vocabulary.
Social incompetence—difficulty relating to others, lack of social amenities.

Some of these deficiencies may be caused by the specific nature of the neurological damage. Or the cause may be traced to lack of training or improper training. The instructional viewpoints and methods outlined in this book were gained from practical experience and the program has been planned to work, regardless of the source of the deficiencies which the child exhibits. However, one must expect that the speed with which a child progresses through the program will be determined by both that nature and severity of the child's involvement and the lack of prior training.

OBJECTIVES OF THE FUNCTIONAL TEACHING PROGRAM

The educational program for mentally retarded children must have as its aim the development of skills and attitudes which will enable the child to participate more fully in activities in his home, institution, and community. Any such program must be concerned not only with specific bits of knowledge but also, and perhaps more importantly, with those skills and attitudes which will be helpful in the ever changing circumstances of his life. This will require that the program do all it can to improve the child's ability to learn, to increase his awareness of his environment, to teach him what he can and cannot do, to develop a reasonable degree of self-discipline, and to help him to become sensitive to the needs and rights of others.

The educational goals for *trainable* children are often described within such categories as self-care, socialization, and expression (e.g., Perry, 34). These categories overlap, but indeed attention must be paid to (a) developing adequate habits of moving about, taking care of one's safety and health; (b) interacting with other people; behaving toward others in acceptable ways, and (c) developing ways of enjoyment, such as participation in games, music, etc. Within each category there are many specific goals toward which children may be led. The reader will note that each exercise described in this book has objectives which fit into these categories. In some cases, an exercise will have several goals. Again, the overall goal of this teaching program is to help the child develop *toward normality*. The extent to which each child will be helped is often unpredictable. All we propose is that this program can be a help in realizing a more satisfactory life for the mentally defective child.

SPECIFIC OBJECTS

Up to this point, we have been discussing rather broad objectives. More specific objectives, as applied in the Laradon Hall program, might be the development of the following abilities: (a) to receive impressions and later to translate these impressions into thought; (b) to act in response to these thoughts and impressions (which, as the program progresses, grow in complexity); (c) to make use of accidentally discovered facts; (d) to apply trial and error; (e) to think logically, and (f) to draw feasible conclusions from logical thought.

TEACHING PRINCIPLES AND PRACTICES

To help attain the objectives mentioned above, to facilitate learning, and to utilize the instructional units most wisely, the following general principles and practices should be followed:

1. A high level of stimulation must be provided. This should include the kind and variety of stimulation which will arouse interest in the child and will necessitate his responding to the stimulation.
2. Provide the highly distractible child with inconspicuous,

calm direction. If necessary, such a child may be separate
from the group temporarily, not as punishment but as
means to reduce the number of distractions.

3. Require that children make decisions in many situations
These should not be dangerous situations or situations in
which it is difficult to make decisions, but the child frequently must be forced into making simple decisions in
the course of ordinary activities.

4. Provide many situations in which the child must differentiate, compare, and match various items, that is, situations in which these operations convey to the learner the
correctness or incorrectness of his response.

5. Rote learning should, when possible, be avoided in favor
of integrating new tasks with previous knowledge or
skills. Since this is not always possible, rote learning may
be sometimes acceptable.

6. Expose the child to events which will help him to perceive causality, particularly to perceive the effects his own
actions have upon various events and objects.

7. Increase the demands made on the child as improvement
occurs.

8. Maintain an understanding, strict discipline. Gradual
efforts should be made to encourage self-discipline.

9. Give rewards freely and promptly for good performances
only. Ordinarily, rewards in the form of general verbal
praise are sufficient.

10. Devise tasks which are appropriate to each child's mental
and physical ability. This may require, at times, use of
special aids, or again, starting a task at a simplified level.

11. A child's physical disabilities, as well as his mental deficiencies, must be worked with. Special exercises, helpful
in the case of physical disability, may also contribute to
the child's confidence, as well as to the improvement of
basic skills needed for mental development.

12. Alternate freely, with sensitivity to the condition of the
child, periods of work, play and rest.

13. Train the child to adjust to and interact with other

children. It seems helpful to develop a "group spirit" or loyalty to other members of his class.

14. The children must be given many opportunities to express their needs for activity. With apathetic children, the teacher must create an increased need for activity.
15. Children should be exposed to many situations outside the school premises.
16. To eliminate undesirable behavior, attempt to substitute desirable habits.
17. Drill periods should be relatively short to avoid loss of attention and possible boredom.
18. Frequently, recreation periods should be used to apply the skills and knowledge being acquired in the classroom.
19. Remember that successful experiences, even the smallest achievements, are more helpful to learning than failure.

Chapter 2

METHODS AND MEANS OF FUNCTIONAL TEACHING

INTRODUCTION

THE IDEA OF A TOTAL overall training program at Laradon Hall was delimited by the imminent needs of the pupils and is only indirectly associated with the knowledge of normal human development. There was not, at the outset, a comprehensive program which dealt with general and specific teaching problems. Through experience, through trial and error, procedures were developed and the various teaching techniques, methods and devices employed in the teaching program.

DEVELOPMENT OF DEVICES UTILIZED IN FUNCTIONAL TEACHING

The functional teaching exercises were developed as the needs of various children became apparent. If a child could not perform adequately a certain action, Mr. McGlone would set out to devise some means to help the child improve his skill. Later, when another skill was found to be lacking, he sought a technique or an apparatus which would help to develop that skill. In this way, he created exercises which consistently helped the child to learn more and more adequate behavior. Thus, more than a hundred and eighty devices were developed which at first were rather specific in application (though it was observed that some devices accomplished more than was expected). It seems to us, upon considering all the exercises, that they can be classified into four major types: those with motor emphasis, others which aim at elementary perceptual development, some for advanced perceptual training, and those with a motor-perceptual coordination emphasis. These divisions resulted from observations which indicated that an individual child exhibited shortcomings falling into one or the other, or into several of these developmental anomalies. That is, some were connected with the areas of motor activities, some with perceptual abilities, and some with motor-perceptual coordination.

Let us now single out one particular device and follow its evolution. We shall use as an example an apparatus for motor training, the so-called **Offset Tires** (**D-16**). The task is to roll these tires according to directions given by the teacher. In the initial version of this task, the child simply rolled an ordinary automobile tire, which provided him with an opportunity to exercise various portions of his body in conjunction with perceptual information. Then Mr. McGlone thought of adding a concrete slab as weight to the inside of the tire at a particular point. This caused the tire to roll erratically and the child had to make rapid adjustments in order to keep up with the tire. This made greater demands on visual-motor coordination and encouraged the child to act and to act quickly under circumstances of rapid change. However, small children had difficulty managing these heavy and clumsy auto tires. Consequently, Mr. McGlone designed a hollow hoop made of metal or plastic which had, on the inside circumference, a screw-in plug through which shot could be put. This shot, acting as an off-center weight, was enclosed in a small compartment inside the hoop. By varying the amount of shot the motions of the hoop could be made more or less erratic. Each of these evolutionary stages was successful in itself and each new version was, in some way, an improvement on the earlier version. It is in this way that many of the devices have been developed and, in a larger view, even the total teaching program.

PRINCIPLES UNDERLYING DEVELOPMENT OF DEVICES

As indicated earlier, the emphasis on motor and perceptual training is the most important aspect of this program. There may be, of course, some doubt as to the wisdom of this emphasis. All one can say in defense of this approach is this: one is working with children whose motor and perceptual development is so impaired that life is for them exceedingly difficult and far from normal. If, then, the training program alleviates these deficiencies, not only is the child able, as a consequence, to behave more adequately but, in addition, his opportunities for further learning are enhanced.

There is another argument which would favor an emphasis on motor-perceptual training. In addition, this argument would favor the order of training that is incorporated in McGlone's program. This is the notion that normal human development follows the scheme: motor to perceptual, to integrated motor-perceptual, and finally to interrelated conceptual skills. Note that this order corresponds to the order of the instructional program followed at Laradon Hall where the greatest emphasis is placed on the first three stages. Basically, the program is intended to supply those experiences, important to normal development, which the mentally retarded child has not had. Further, these experiences along with the motor activities are arranged in such a way that the child, on achieving success at one exercise, can move forward to another exercise.

We find that there are few comprehensive or systematic instructional programs for trainable retarded children. Special classes in the public schools as well as in private institutions often revise an existing curriculum for normal students in a way that may meet some of the special needs of retarded students, or borrow ideas relevant to the field from many different sources. Sometimes the teachers devise procedures of their own to get along in any way possible. These methods most often result in a compilation of unrelated teaching units. The merit of the program devised at Laradon Hall is that it is a continuous program with a central rationale, namely, that of teaching the student according to a behavioral developmental sequence.

In developing the instructional program described in this book, it soon became apparent that diversification of activities was an important need. Let us take *locomotion* as an example and elaborate. A student handicapped by poor or inadequate locomotion will, in the course of the program, be subjected to as great a range and variety of locomotion experiences as possible. It is understood, of course, that his musculature is functional, but that he has not learned how, or has not been able to use it properly. The training starts at an elementary level, is continually expanded, elaborated and made more complex. In this way the pupil may learn to locomote under various conditions, at various speeds, and in many ways, such as by walking, hopping, crawling, skipping, running, etc. Experience indicates that activity in quantity only is rather pointless. For example, if day after day, a child continually repeats a given action, such as walking a certain pattern laid out on the floor, he eventually learns to perform this specific activity satisfactorily; but if later he should be called upon to perform a similar and related, but not identical activity, he often will fail. Though he has certainly expended a great amount of time and energy to acquire the particular skill, he may have learned only that special skill and not how to locomote satisfactorily in general. So, when faced with different locomotion requirements, he is unable to perform the new activities, either immediately or after short practice. For this reason, diversification of exercises is stressed.

IMPLICATIONS FOR THE LEARNING PROCESS

It might not be out of place here to say a few general words about the learning process in human beings. Much of the knowledge or skill acquired prior to the planned learning process is learned in a manner which can be called incidental, accidental, unformalized, casual, or unsystematized. Each one of these terms describes in part such learning. This knowledge should be, and in the normal child's case is, extensive, diverse, and drawn from the environment and the materials that form the child's world. Every educator will agree that this prior learning is a foundation for any future learning in the classroom. Each child who enters school for the first time brings his own individual experiential aggregations with him. Yet most children enter school for the first time on a somewhat comparable basis since they have shared a common cultural experience background.

However, discrepancies will occur. A child, for instance may not, for one reason or another, have had experience in some specific areas of life. Consequently, upon entering school, he has not acquired the appropriate *readiness,* which may show up in motor and perceptual deficiencies. An extreme example of this type of child would be the educationally deprived children mentioned throughout history, who probably were rejected and expelled as babies because they displayed retardation. The possibility that the fact that in the preschool years normal experiences fail to occur will account for the slow learner's difficulties, has been explored by Kephart (24).

There is a considerable lack of knowledge regarding what is commonly learned and what can be learned in the first five years of human life. Some experts list specific behaviors acquired by young children in these years but there has been little attempt to classify these behaviors in any rational system. Kephart (24) has made the point that through motor activity of any type the infant child first experiences his environment. Later perceptual learning proceeds out of sensory experiences parallel with, and in some cases produced by motor activities. After this phase, motor-perceptual (or perceptual-motor) integration begins to take place. This concept of developmental sequence is similar to the one on which is based the sequential approach of the teaching methodology used in Functional Teaching.

In the following chapters, 4 to 7, a more detailed discussion will take place. Here will be found an explanation of the four stages within the program and a description of the various underlying behavioral themes. In addition, we shall endeavor to show how the devices and methods used are intended to aid the child in learning to perform a variety of activities and here we shall point out other features pertinent to the teaching procedures.

Chapter 3

THE RELATION OF HISTORICAL AND CONTEMPORARY THEORIES TO FUNCTIONAL TEACHING

INTRODUCTION

THE PROGRAM of functional teaching developed at Laradon Hall bears, we believe, many interesting relationships to a number of educational philosophies and practices, both old and new. The program reflects a concern, an emphasis, similar to that which is found in the works of Jean Marc Itard, Edouard Seguin, and Maria Montessori, each of whom, in his work with the mentally retarded, emphasized a combination of motor training and sensory training. In addition, Montessori worked out a scheme for educating normal children which utilized essentially the same approach that Seguin had developed for "defective" children. It is not surprising, although Roy McGlone was not acquainted with the details of these educators' work, that some of his exercises should be very similar to those devised by these earlier workers.

McGlone attributes some of his inspiration to Angelo Mosso and to August Forel, both of whom will be discussed later. It is of interest, too, to note that the functional approach contains some features which resemble B. F. Skinner's operant conditioning approach. Indeed, it seems to us that the didactic exercises of functional teaching, the teaching procedures of Itard, Seguin and Montessori, the neuro-physiological investigations of Mosso and Forel and the conditioning maneuvers used by Skinner in training animals and in programming learning material, have a great deal in common.

Let us recall briefly a few of the major figures whose work appears to be historically related to the teaching program to be described here, and let us consider, too, some of the modern views within the perspective of which may be developed a deeper understanding of the functional teaching approach.

17

JEAN MARC ITARD

In 1801, Jean Marc Itard (20) published his description of the so-called *Wild Boy of Aveyron.* This was probably the first record of a systematic effort to educate a child who fell well below the normal in intelligence. The boy was described by Itard as resembling a wild animal more than a human being, lacking many of those responses normal to a child of his age. In his monumental chronicle, which was to make a significant impact on future developments in the field of education and treatment of the retarded, Itard described his attempt to bring to Victor the benefits of civilization and culture. By providing contrasting sensory stimulation, the young physician was able to imprint some of the elements of culture on this young man.

Believing that it was through sensory functions that knowledge of the environment must be conveyed, Itard proceeded on the notion that only through the sensory functions of the young savage could he prove the relatively more important role of environment over heredity in the eventual development of the individual. Remember that the senses of this boy were reduced to such a state of inertia that the unfortunate creature was quite inferior to some of our domestic animals.

Victor, the Wild Boy, had heretofore only very primitive modes of learning, inadequate for learning how to deal with complex society. Itard sought, through exercise of the senses, to provide Victor with the tools necessary to gain knowledge of his environment. Without this *modus operandi* there would have been little in the way of systematic education in prospect for this savage. Itard realized not only the need to develop the sensory functions, but also, the corresponding need to develop in this savage an awareness of the uses that could be made of the senses. This Itard attempted to achieve by subjecting Victor to greatly contrasting stimuli, overlooking no means or avenues of acquiring or exploring sensory information in the process. Eventually, Victor appeared to obtain a rudimentarily human outlook upon the world about him.

Itard recognized that it was essential to stimulate and exercise the sensory avenues: the boy was dunked in hot water baths and then exposed to cold water immediately following the baths; foul smelling materials were contrasted with pleasant smelling ones; loud sounds were followed by soft ones. However, this stimulation of the sensory avenues, he was convinced, was not enough. To refine their function was equally essential and it is this refinement and development of the sensory modalities which constitute the most important elements of Itard's approach. Progressively these sharply different stimulations were made more similar so that greater discrimination was required. As these refinements took place Victor approximated more and more the image of the so-called socialized person.

This was not a smooth process. It was constantly necessary for the physician to check his efforts against the behavior of the boy and, on many occasions, to shift directions in order to circumvent obstacles to his intended educational goals.

Itard, after working for a considerable length of time, came to believe his goals for Victor to be unattainable and ended his experiment. However, though his work was finished, there remained his dynamic thesis: that the potentialities of the retarded individual are often measured in terms of the potentiality of his gaining from a method of teaching or treatment. The success or failure of any method of teaching or treating such a person are, to a great extent, dependent upon the knowledge that supports and underlies these endeavors. Yet, the documentation of his experiences not only constituted a great legacy left by this patient and incredible physician but demonstrated incontrovertibly that something could be done for the retarded. Greater knowledge and understanding would undoubtedly have suggested additional means of attacking this problem. The more we know and understand the retarded individual the greater *his* potential.

EDOUARD SEGUIN

The tremendous possibilities of Itard's work became evident to his student, Edouard Seguin (41) . In the course of his medical training under Dr. Itard, Seguin became caught up with some of the purposes of Itard's work with Voctor. By carrying these ideas further, and integrating them with his own, Seguin developed what he called a physiological approach to teaching the mentally retarded.

Seguin advocated the *bombardment* of the central nervous system through sensory stimulation. This led to his less explicit notion that such stimulation might develop the process of association, a procedure which should, in turn, lead the child to gain more from his experiences (in themselves sensory experiences). Pursuing this train of thought further, it seemed likely that the senses themselves would be brought to function more effectively. Thus it was suggested that a maturational effect is produced through the total development of the sensory modalities. It must be remembered that Seguin's position was developed within the context of the notion of a *blocked* or damaged nervous system. Present day theory with respect to retraining of certain essential nervous system functions would seem to give new impetus to Seguin's position.

The specific value of the physical training advocated by Seguin often has been overlooked. His deliberate disordering of the equilibrium leads to an adjustment on the part of the child of these disordered motions, a process calculated to promote orderly movements. The results of his studies suggested, as do the results of the study upon which this book is based, that it is precisely in the nature of these intentionally disordered motions or disequilibriums that neuro-physiologically oriented goals for the retarded individual can be attained. This involves an awareness of bodily movements, the partial or total control of which is the eventual desired outcome of these procedures, and indicates a sensorially based awareness of one's total repertoire of movements. (Note that a lack of awareness in the mentally retarded child is suggested in the writings of Seguin. That this lack of awareness is neuro-physiologically based is also suggested.)

With many other educators, Seguin advocated that training be initially concerned with major generalized motor movement and subsequently, with specific finer motor movement. With respect to the latter, this physician-teacher's preoccupation with what could be called hand training might be considered a precursor of a more modern concept of perceptual-motor coordination.

Modern theories of teaching retarded children reflect more and more the emphasis placed on sensory exploration, or curiosity, in Seguin's program. The importance of this emphasis has, in the past, often been overlooked.

MARIA MONTESSORI

It remained for Dr. Deteressa Maria Montessori (29) to advance the work of Seguin. Montessori, impressed with the work of Seguin, utilized much of his neuro-physiological approach. The sensory training of Itard and Seguin found a place in the Montessori Method. Such training is intended to provide a sensory awareness and a utilization of the sensory modalities to gain knowledge about the environment or, to put it another way, to gain a *modus operandi* for learning. Montessori was concerned with these processes on a neuro-physiological level and through her experiences came to believe that mental development is achieved by the interaction of the individual with his environment. She recognized that the child's ability to note likenesses and differences lies at the base of his ability to form associations and to make judgments. That there be stimulation and contrasts between stimuli, she believed, is not enough. The child must be taught to make judgments based on perceptions of likenesses and differences at increasing levels of difficulty. In her work, the emphasis was largely on visual and auditory discrimination, although the development of discriminations requiring the use of other senses was also encouraged.

Montessori's thinking led her to incorporate into her teaching devices features which would assure or increase the likelihood, not only that the child would have to discriminate, but that he would be immediately informed of the correctness of his judgments. (We can see a present day parallel in the modern teaching machine.) These teaching objectives now appear to play a vastly important role in the development of perception and in some cases, of concepts in the retarded child.

The orderly development of concepts was another important concern for Montessori. Standing (47, pp. 146, 147) points out that in the Montessori Method:

> The process of abstraction depends on two factors, both of which must be present. The first is that there must be absolute clarity in the concrete. And the second is that the child must have reached a certain maturity of mind. . . . A . . . danger . . . is that of hustling on the child's mind, and forcing it to do sums in the abstract before it has formed a clear notion of the operation in the concrete. . . . The child's mind—in order to rise into the abstract—needs first to move in contact with the solid and concrete.

It is a characteristic of the Montessori approach that the child must meet the demands of one level before being allowed to proceed to a higher level. This has the value of permitting the child to progress at his own rate and prevents the progress of one child from interfering with that of another.

This emphasis on formality was among those practices criticized in America by advocates of the so-called progressive approach to education. In some respects, the abandonment in this country of her scheme as it was applied later to normal children had the effect of obscuring its potential for the retarded child, for whom it was originally conceived. The exploration of these resources is yet to be undertaken.

ANGELO MOSSO

Mosso (30), a renowned authority on fatigue, provided information which may be of value to the field of education of the retarded child. His studies (1915) regarding attention and concentration of attention (as it related to fatigue) appear to be particularly related to this discussion. Mosso sought to understand the physiological mechanisms of attention and concentration. His discussion of attention as a process with a neurophysiological basis suggests that it is connected with the thought processes.

The writings of Mosso indicate that attention is related to motor phenomena which leads to the suggestion that movement is also a part of attenton. This author does not explore the complications or implications of damage to the central nervous system with respect to concentration and attention but his work in isolating these phenomena is nonetheless of great importance.

Of significance to those who are desirous of finding ways to educate the retarded child is Mosso's contribution to the understanding of the physiological basis of the thought processes. Thought processes appear to be mediated, among other ways, by *attention* and *concentration*. These latter, in turn, may be related to the acquisition of those understandings which the child needs for effective learning. It must be appreciated that in the mentally retarded child there may be interference in these thought (cognitive) processes which can be attributed to whatever etiology of the mental retardation and which call for special techniques for imparting these understandings.

The teacher may be specifically interested in the areas of attention and concentration because of their relationship to the thought processes. A thorough knowledge of these two functions is basic to the understanding of a child's learning behavior and learning needs. Increased knowledge concerning the nature of attention and concentration, for example, permits the educator to formulate teaching goals and teaching maneuvers designed to focus on these areas.

In utilizing the ideas of Mosso, McGlone apparently gave a great deal of consideration to the physiological implications of attention, concentration and the thought processes as they supplemented his knowledge, gained through observation, of children with possible central nervous system impairment.

AUGUST FOREL

The views of the Swiss physician and psychologist Forel (10) parallel those of the contemporary Kephart (24) and Strauss and Kephart (49) with respect to perceptual-motor training. This early work (1907) suggested that the central nervous system is responsible for comparing the symbols—the sensations and perceptions—of one sense with those of another and that through this comparison errors correct themselves.

This author also suggests the phenomenon of "muscle

memory" (see Chapter 7). This appears to be an important factor in certain perceptual-motor and physical training outcomes.

ALICE DESCOEUDRES

Some aspects of Dr. Montessori's work were further developed by another notable educator. Alice Descoeudres (6), a teacher, worked with retarded children in Belgium. Kirk and Johnson (22) give her credit for practicing many modern theories of education.

For purposes of this discussion, her distinct contributions are her further applications of the sensory and physical training approaches as advocated by Montessori. Among her other accomplishments, she developed what was called the "object lesson" for subnormal children. These object lessons are credited with being forerunners of the "units of experience" which are familiar in modern curricula for the educable retarded.

The modern student should not overlook another important contribution by this teacher, namely, the implicit connection between the sensory training and the object lessons. She came to believe that through the sensory training the child was prepared for the conditions under which his unit of experience or object lesson would take place. The importance of this contribution can be better appreciated if we remember that this author was interested in the development of a program for children with a deficit in the perceptual processes. It appears that sensory training increases the possibility of the desired experiences occurring, and these experiences, in turn, further increase the probability of the formation of a more effective sensory facilitation of experience. It is particularly apparent in the manner in which this author combines the sensory experiences with what we would call *content,* as happens in the case of the object lesson.

LISE GELLNER

This physician contemporary (13) has described a differential diagnosis and a general system of classification directed toward the specific areas of visual and auditory perceptual involvement in mentally retarded children. This procedure has important implications for methods of teaching children with these types of deficiencies. Of great significance is the underlying principle that in teaching the retarded, the affected area can be circumvented, and the teaching accomplished via work with the nonaffected areas.

Future developments in her work may reveal more specific considerations such as the suggestion that certain teaching methods may be indicated in some cases and contraindicated in others.

Gellner describes four kinds of perceptual integrative dysfunction resulting from injury to this region: visuo-somatic (motor), visuo-autonomic, auditory-somatic (motor), and auditory-autonomic. The visuo-somatic group has an impairment affecting the integration of visual and proprioceptive (somatic) impulses. This defect is functionally manifested as movement blindness. Clinically the children are described as hypoactive with difficulty in making visual contact with the environment due to impairment of visuo-kinetic faculties of seeing. The visuo-autonomic group has an impairment affecting the integration of visual and interoceptive (autonomic) impulses. The defect is functionally manifested as meaning blindness. Clinically the children are described as hyperactive with difficulty in grasping and responding intelligently to visual environment. The auditory-somatic group has an impairment affecting the integration of auditory and proprioceptive (somatic) impulses. The defect shows functionally as word-sound deafness. Clinically the children are described as speechless or speech defective with difficulty in making verbal contact due to impairment of somatic faculties of speech and hearing. Finally the auditory-autonomic group has an impairment affecting the integration of auditory and interoceptive (autonomic) impulses. Functionally the defect is manifested as word-meaning deafness. Clinically the children are described as showing psychotic appearing behavior with parrot speech and with difficulty in using language intelligently due to lacking powers of grasping the meaning of words. In practice one observes combinations of syndromes and not just symptoms belonging to one group exclusively.

* * * *

The main contribution of Gellner consists of the attempt to identify, isolate, and describe clinical syndromes in relation to their neuropsychiatric, educational and pathological manifestations. Her views on the significance of the relationship between learning disabilities and perceptual neurologic dysfunctions, the importance of diagnosing such defects before any engagement in training, the emphasis on vigorous training through social interaction and on using intact perceptual-sensory pathways as routes of communication in remedial instruction, are sound and deserve careful attention of medical clinicians, educators and clinical psychologists.

The neuropathological conditions described by Gellner belong to a large group of disorders which are otherwise summarily called the organic brain syndrome or the syndrome of neurologic impairment of the central nervous system function.

Organic brain syndrome and neurologic impairment is a condition resulting from injury to the central nervous system before, during or after birth of a child. The injury occurs during a period of intense growth and is, therefore, combined with serious maldevelopmental manifestations. Clinically, one distinguishes between acute and chronic neurological conditions. The mentally deficient children seen in the classroom or in institutions are usually victims of the chronic syndrome resulting from permanent, irreversible diffuse impairment of the central nervous system's tissue function. The severity of the syndrome varies in accordance with the severity of damage. The symptoms depend on the location, the extensiveness, and the time of the occurrence of injury. Behavioral, personality, neurotic and psychotic disorders are usually superimposed upon the original brain damage. The neurologic impairment may vary in degree from severe to minimal and may be characterized by mental deficiency; by difficulty in comprehension, perception, orientation, memory, thinking, learning and judgment; by defects in the visual, auditory, tactile and kinesthetic sensation; by motor disabilities such as spastic paralysis, athetosis, dystonia, choreiform movements, myoclonic movements, tremors, hypokinesis, hyperkinesis; by convulsive disorders; by short attention span and distractibility; and by various emotional reactions. (5, Hundziak)

B. F. SKINNER

It seems to us that the teaching methods described in this book contain a number of the features emphasized by Skinner (44) in his work on operant conditioning and programmed learning. The Functional Teaching method insists that there be some behavior toward which the training is leading. The steps toward the desired behavior must be successively more exacting approximations of that behavior. Generous praise, i.e., reinforcement, is given for success but not necessarily for every success. It seems to us that in Skinner's terms, McGlone's schedules of reinforcements, because they do not correlate 100 per cent with successful behavior, are distributed in a variable interval fashion. It should be noted that Functional Teaching practitioners are enthusiastic about rewarding a child's successful performance, but will not reward what they see as a failure. Also, there seem to be efforts to build into the child a self-reinforcement process, i.e., the child by knowing very explicitly what is expected of him, can by living up to that expectation know, himself, that he has been successful.

NEWELL C. KEPHART

It remained for Kephart (24) to elaborate on theories, practices and procedures and suggest the importance of sensory-motor awareness. The sensory awareness, through the mediation of the muscular sense, of one's body and one's place in space has been shown to be crucial to the formation of an adequate self or bodily image. An adequate bodily image also requires the motor act: physical movements of all kinds including the act of propelling oneself through space (e.g., walking) .

This concept can be correlated with Kephart's thinking regarding the role of motion or movement in the thought processes. He suggests that through certain maneuvers, carried out in specific physical training techniques, the retarded child is enabled to engage in mental functions not ordinarily expected of him.

Kephart (24) stresses the importance of perceptual-motor *matching* as an educational concern. Strauss and Kephart (49) describe responses to a stimulus situation as a "coordination of numbers of responses synchronized with the coordinated stimulus

pattern which he (the child) perceives." The *feedback* phenomenon herein suggested appears to be related to both sensory and
physical training.

The process of conceptual development, according to Kephart,
requires on the part of the retarded child the ability to deal with
similarities and differences. Strauss and Kephart discussed the role
that the perception of likenesses and differences plays in the basic
conceptual processes. According to Kephart, learning gaps caused
by failure in the perceptual-motor matching process appear to
have major implications for the education of the retarded child.

It is germane to the theme of this text to point out, in the
words of Strauss and Kephart that:

> In the development of any organism, the parts subserve the whole
> and we cannot correctly think of the parts except in their relationship
> to the whole. When we trace the development of a part, as in the
> nervous system, we must not allow ourselves to consider that what
> we observe in its development exists alone. Rather, we must at all
> times remember that this particular development that we are observ-
> ing has only the purpose of contributing toward the whole, and its
> development will be modified and altered to serve the demands of the
> whole of which it is a part.

It should also be noted that these authors reflect that, especially in the case of retarded brain-injured children where perception
is frequently grossly impaired, we must make every effort to increase the efficiency of the most impaired sense rather than to
attempt to substitute another sense modality. Hence the extreme
importance of visual perceptual training in the brain-injured
child.

MARIANNE FROSTIG

This worker in the field has been responsible for materials
on remediation techniques in the area of perception. Based on
clinical observations of children with learning difficulties, she
developed the widely used Developmental Test of Visual Perception (12). The differentiation of various kinds of visual-
perceptual abilities is one of its chief aims.

The remediation program is in six developmental areas:
sensory-motor abilities, language, visual and auditory perception,

higher thought processes, social adjustment and emotional development.

The identification of some of the visual perceptual learning problems of children has been of considerable value in educational programming for the developmentally disabled.

CONCLUSION

The reader is by now aware that many of the contributors cited here have some connection with the teaching practices of Roy McGlone at Laradon Hall. In some cases he has cited his obligations, in others he has been unaware of any direct influence. It is obvious that McGlone was able to arrive at some principles independently and that he was also able to utilize ideas. He was able to discover and recombine meaningful components in the work of many of the earlier contributors. He was able to organize these elements into a workable scheme, adding and eliminating as each development proved or did not prove successful. By constant and sensitive reflection he was able to weed out the less useful procedures and to strengthen the more effective ones. By keen discernment and creative techniques he was able to formulate principles of his own from which still newer principles emerged.

An attempt has been made in this chapter to point up, through the literature in special education and psychology developments which appear to coincide with or support the program at Laradon Hall. It is hoped that these will assist in clarifying and giving broader dimension to principles and practices presented in this volume.

Chapter 4

TEACHING MOTOR ACTIVITIES

INTRODUCTION

A LARGE PART OF THE PROGRAM that is described here is intended primarily to improve the child's ability to locomote, maintain balance, spatially orient himself, breathe properly, move rhythmically, and perform fine movements with reasonable precision. All these activities are important in their own right. In addition, we believe that an early emphasis in the training program upon motor activity is fundamental to the later development of perceptual and conceptual skills. Such a belief is consistent with several different points of view, e.g., those of Edouard Seguin, Jean Piaget, J. B. Watson, and Newell C. Kephart.

A major problem in working with many retarded children lies in the apathy which pervades so much of their lives. Just getting some mentally retarded children to do anything is very difficult. Undoubtedly this behavior problem can be caused by many factors. Apathy can be caused by a variety of anatomical and physiological anomalies which may resist direct efforts at treatment. On the other hand, apathy can develop as a result of and as a way of coping with failure or as a result of the lack of stimulation required to instigate activity. Regardless of the causes of apathy, and in the absence of medical contra indications, many of the exercises reported here may be used to increase the child's activity level. The results of increasing the activity of apathetic children may be better health, finer muscle tone, and increased vigor. In addition, the increased activity may help to broaden the range of effective stimulation of the child, increase the possibilities for learning and improve his morale. If we are convinced that this world contains many things of potential interest to the retarded apathetic child, our first task often will be that of instigating activity on his part, that is motor, sensory, and perceptual activities.

The general principles followed in developing the motor exercises and devices described here have been: (a) each exercise must be planned so that action on the child's part is necessary; (b) exercises should be interesting to the child and (c) demands made on the child should increase as his activity increase and as activity increases and as his skill improves.

It should be noticed that many of the exercises described here may contribute to the child's growing awareness of *cause and effect* relationships. Very often one notices that mentally retarded children are only dimly aware of what they can do with their bodies and of the consequences of their activities. Deliberate efforts to teach the perception of causal relationships should be a challenging problem for teachers of the retarded. We shall mention some exercises here whose primary function is to teach the perception of causality. It will be wise for the teacher to utilize each exercise as much as possible, in a manner that may contribute to increasing the child's skill in perceiving the relationship of his own activities to other events which may have been effected by his activities.

LOCOMOTION, BALANCE AND SPATIAL ORIENTATION

These three types of activities are emphasized in the motor training phase. All kinds of locomotor functions are required to use many of the specific devices. The manipulation of some of the apparatuses utilizes extensive and/or general locomotion, others develop precise movements, and some exercise both types of activity. In the Laradon Hall program, these two skills are regarded as the most significant parts of proper motor development, as they are vital to motion, locomotion and the total physical bearing. Many balance activities are referred to as *neuro-equilibrium* activities. This term is suggested by their tendency to purposely induce a temporary state of disequilibrium requiring and evoking compensating and adjustive responses. Related to this discussion is the work of Kephart (24) with respect to *laterality and directionaly*. "Laterality is an internal awareness of the two sides of the body and their difference." Quoting this author further, "When the child has developed laterality within his own organism and is aware of the right and left sides of his own body, he is ready to project these directional concepts into external space" (directionality).

The term *positionality* used later in this book is based on the above author's discussion of postural adjustment.

Among the devices used at Laradon Hall, which are relevant to this discussion, are the following:

Stepping Ladder	A-14
Balance Beam (with Mirror)	A-7
Snail	D-7
Stepping Blocks	C-47
Table Swing	A-8
Treadmill	A-16
Sinking Tires	A-9
Climbing Obstacle	A-10
Crawling Maze	A-5
Swinging Tunnel	A-11
Caterpillar (Tractor)	D-15
Horizontal Ladders	A-12

For an example of an outdoor arrangement for these devices, see Part II. An instructional film on these and other devices is available (see McGlone 28a).

BREATHING

Breathing, or respiration, is an aspect of motor training that is often neglected. Yet it is necessary to any proper training program and is a prerequisite to further motor training.

From our observation it seems that many mentally retarded people have shallow breathing and consequently little stamina. (We know of no studies of breathing practices among the mentally retarded, but proper breathing does not necessarily come naturally.) Also, in addition to developing proper breathing, the techniques cited below are used to hasten physical relaxation after taking part in some fatiguing activity. Thus, the breathing exercises described here have two purposes: they are used to increase the likelihood of the child breathing properly as he engages in srenuous activity; they are used as an aid to relaxation following exercise. The techniques used are the *Suction Blocks* (**A-15**) and the *Bottled Odors* (**B-2**).

RHYTHM

Rhythm is a characteristic of coordination that is important to smooth motor functioning and to economy of body motion. Rhythmic movement is emphasized in some of the exercises and, in the case of many of the exercises, is expected to improve with experience. When the child learns to perform the exercises with smoothly flowing motions it can be assumed that he is ready to move on to further training.

Rhythm is also an essential factor in the extensions of the motor training program, such as folk-dancing, roller-skating, swimming and gymnastic activity. The devices that are particularly effective in the establishment of rhythmic activity appear to be the **Back and Forth Seesaw** (**A-18a**) and the **Lateral Seesaw** (**A-18b**). **Singing** (**C-26**), of course, is an activity that requires and, hopefully, promotes rhythm.

PRECISION AND AGILITY

On many of the motor training devices, fairly gross activity constitutes the major indication of achievement. However, with some of the devices a fair degree of agility and precise movement is demanded. The child need not become an expert on these exercises, but any progress is to be valued. The physical requirements are dependent upon motor activity already learned. The exercises have the common feature either of being games or of providing amusement as well as motor training. Some of the games may be played by two or more individuals. Competition, when used without the consequent hazard of humiliation, may be a part of many exercises. They can also be considered as repetitive applications of earlier training. The devices belonging in this category are the **Barber Pole** (**B-34**), **Table Shuffleboard** (**C-39**), and **Junior Jai-Alai** (**D-13**).

CAUSE AND EFFECT

Some of the motor exercises can teach a child something about cause and effect relationships. When we speak of *cause and effect* we refer specifically to the causal physical relationships which exist between the child's activities and certain features of the various didactic devices. Such relationships may consist of the child doing something to a device which then does something "startling" by itself; or the child does something to a device in which engenders curiosity and then does something "startling" back to the child. Devices which aim at cause and effect and learning to react via a startle stimulus are ***Water Pump*** (**A-6**), ***Table Swing*** (**A-8**), ***Noise Cage*** (**B-26**), ***Bell Ringing*** (**B-27**), and ***Wired Hose*** (**A-2**).

RECREATION AND OTHER EXTENSIONS

There are several exercises in this program which do not use specially designed devices. Many of these exercises are considered as extensions of the motor training program. They include such activities as **Singing (C-26)**, **Folk Dancing (D-4)**, **Swimming Tables (C-31)**, **Gymnasium Games (D-6)**, and **Roller Skating (D-5)**. All of these activities, even singing, may be dependent, more or less, upon applications of motor efficiency which have been acquired through earlier exercises. Most of these activities can be done either with individual students or in groups.

Chapter 5

INITIAL PERCEPTUAL TRAINING

INTRODUCTION

THE PREVIOUS CHAPTER was principally concerned with the methods and devices that contribute to improving motor skills. In this chapter we shall be mainly concerned with sensory-perceptual training.

SENSATION AND PERCEPTION

In all activities (if the organs are operational and the nervous system is functional) there are sensational elements and, often, related perceptions. The perceptual impression may or may not be accurately related to the sensory data. The relationship of sensation to perception may depend upon many variables such as degree and purity of sensory stimulation, prior experience, length of sensory excitation, etc. When a severely retarded person does not respond overtly to sensory stimulation, there is the possibility that perceptual interpretation of the sensory data is not occurring or is occurring in a distorted fashion. Consequently, it is felt that systematic sensory stimulation must be provided in a fashion which will initiate perceptual interpretation. It is further felt that, with many of the children, most activity with each device begins at the sensory level and then takes on perceptual meaning, especially with the devices used at the outset of the training program. In order to further clarify the relationship between sensation and perception we shall mention four devices: *Feathers and Honey* (A-1), *Chasing Mirror Reflections* (A-4), the *Noise Cage* (B-26), and *Bell Ringing* (B-27).

VISION

Vision is a sense modality through which we gain a great deal of our information about the world. With no vision, or with poor vision, a person is at a great disadvantage. Thus, retarded children who do not utilize visual experiences are at a considerable disadvantage. This program includes many exercises which demand that the visual sense to be used to discriminate, identify, compare, and match. Examples would be: *Separation of Objects A* (**B-4**), *Separation of Objects B* (**B-5**), *Pattern Matching A* (**C-8**), *Pattern Matching B* (**C-9**), *Pattern Matching C,* (**C-10**), the *Opaque Projector* (**C-25**), the *All Around Device (Calliope)* (**B-20**), the *Colored Nail Board* (**C-17**), *Colored Yarns, Shaded* (**B-9**), *Framed Inset Puzzles* (**C-1**), *Inset Puzzles* (**B-10**), and *Skull Pairing* (**B-16**), There are many other devices that utilize visual discrimination which will be considered in the next chapter.

AUDITION

Among mentally retarded children there are both those who have functional hearing losses which contribute to their retardation and those who either cannot or do not heed auditory stimulation. The first group may be aided greatly by speech therapists. However, the second group who, structurally, have adequate organs, need to be approached in a different manner. In a general sense, it seems that they have never learned *how* to hear effectively. Consequently, the approach would seem to be one of special instruction. The approach used in Functional Teaching is to purposely place the child in hearing situations where he is first compelled by the nature of the stimuli to pay attention to them, and then to get meaning out of them. Later he is confronted with very specific auditory discrimination exercises. This training is integrated with speech therapy for it is well known that speech disorders of various sorts often are associated with various types of hearing difficulties.

For the children who have normal hearing, the emphasis, in the auditory training exercises, is placed on the development of the child's awareness of sounds and his ability to discriminate more carefully between sounds. Some of the devices that are used in training auditory attention and discrimination are: the *Noise Cage* (**B-26**), *Bell Ringing* (**B-27**), *Masks and Bells* (**B-28**), the *All Around Device (Calliope)* (**B-20**), *Sound Matching* (**B-29**), the *Carillon Pipes* (**B-30**), and *Tone Counting* (**B-31**).

OLFACTORY, KINESTHETIC, TACTILE SENSES

The sensory modalities of smell, proprioception, and tactile sensitivity will be considered in one section only, because there are not a great number of devices employed in training within these areas. Perhaps more exercises involving these senses should be developed, although it is generally held that less information is acquired through these sense modalities than is acquired via vision and audition. There is only one device here that is concerned with odor discrimination. There are five devices in this phase of training that emphasize touch and the muscle sense. However, these are considered quite extensively in Chapter 7.

The odor discrimination training device is called *Odors (Bottled Odors)* (**B-2**). The devices that require the exercise of the proprioceptive sense are the: *All Around Device (Calliope)* (**B-20**), *Hidden Objects* (**B-17**), *Colored Nail Board* (**C-17**), and *Weight Matching* (**B-11**). The two devices related to touch training are the *Sand and Dirt Boxes* (**B-1**), and *Hidden Objects* (**B-17**). *Fabric Weaving* (**D-9**) offers an opportunity to develop "muscle memory" (see Chapter 7).

FORM

The process of attending to form involves a child in perceptual activity. He is now combining sensation units into perceptual structures. To have any meaning, various visual elements, such as position, size, texture, color, etc., must be combined some way into a pattern or into what some psychologists call a *gestalt*. Much of form perception requires the utilization of visual experiences, many of which are elementary in nature. Form percepton, too, is often a requirement for the child's spatial orientation. All perceptions, whether complex or relatively simple, must ultimately rely upon the organization by the child of a variety of sensations. Mental retardates frequently have difficulty in doing this. The analysis of this difficulty often reveals that the sensory dysfunctions in these children are individual. Hence, the training program spends a great amount of effort on developing form perception as well as other varieties of perception. At first,

the general approach is to confront the student with exercises
that contain only a relatively few visual elements. As the child's
perceptual processes improve a greater number of sensational
elements are introduced. Though there are, of course, other
devices that also involve some aspect of form perception, we
have listed below eleven exercises that deal explicitly with this
type of perception. These devices are *Writing* (**C-32**), *Hidden
Objects* (**B-17**), *Colored Nail Board* (**C-17**), *Colored Cubes*
(**B-14**), *Framed Inset Puzzles* (**C-1**), *Inset Puzzles* (**B-10**), *Arcs
and Angles* (**B-21**), *Triple Card Matching* (**C-14**), *Mosaic Puzzles*
(**B-18**), *Versatile Sticks (B-35)*, and *Bark Splitting* (**D-3**).

Chapter 6

ADVANCED PERCEPTUAL TRAINING

INTRODUCTION

THE PRECEDING PHASE of the program was concerned with developing appropriate relationships between sensation and perception. This phase deals with more complicated aspects of perception and with the formation of concepts.

In all probability this portion of the program is as important for the so-called *educable* group as it is for the *trainable,* as it may help to prepare the educable child for greater achievement in academic classes. Often, these exercises involve difficult but important steps which the child must learn. They are designed to prepare him to function in various changing situations of life.

There are several sections in this particular training phase. These include learning to rank and match stimuli and to identify letters and simple words. Also included are instructional games, conceptualizing exercises and training extensions. The exercises used during this training phase help to develop the ability to pair, sort and differentiate stimuli; they help children to become more familiar with the symbols needed in arithmetic, reading, writing, and spelling. Later, portions of this phase are specifically concerned with applying the skills mentioned above to games and work.

RANKING

Ranking objects or events is the first and probably one of the simplest conceptual or pre-conceptual activities we will consider. In learning to rank events, the children are learning a basic form of categorizing, that is, the organization and ordering of materials according to such criteria as color, shape, size, etc. It is understood that this is a very elementary form of conceptualizing since it amounts to learning to realize that even differences in events may be ordered in some form. Some of the devices used here are **Weight Matching (B-11)**, **Long and Short (B-12)**, **Carillon Pipes (B-30)**, and **Versatile Sticks (B-35)**.

MATCHING

Matching of various stimuli receives a great amount of attention in the Laradon Hall teaching program. In the matching exercises, the child has an opportunity to note similarities, differences, and groupings among objects and events. It is felt that such demands must be made on the child if we are to expect him to learn to be more aware of his world and to react to it accordingly. The devices named below are the major devices used in this approach: *Colored Yarns* (B-8); *Separation of Objects* (B-4 and B-5); *Pattern Matching* (C-8, C-9, and C-10); *Treasure Hunt* (B-32); *Weight Matching* (B-11); *Sound Matching* (B-29); *Pattern Matching (Food Cards)* (C-11); *Triple Card Matching* (C-14); *Counting Pans* (C-33); *Pattern Matching (Photo Cards)* (C-12); *Word Matching Cards* (C-19); *Number Identification* (C-24); *Sentence Building Frame (C-21)*, and *Skull Pairing* (B-16).

NUMBER IDENTIFICATION AND SYMBOL READINESS

The materials mentioned here are all intended to contribute to the appropriate understanding and use of numbers. In the devices listed below, numbers are recognized, memorized, identified, used in simple counting, used in *life* situations and games, manipulated, and used in special circumstances. Many other devices used in the program, but not mentioned here, involve numbers for recognition or familiarity, as incidental stimuli in conjunction with other activities. Each child is helped to progress as much as he possibly can in learning number and symbol recognition. There is no arbitrary goal set for any child, that is, no one says: "Because this student is pretty slow, let's get him to count to ten and let it go at that." It is expected that some children will eventually gain some insight into counting and the manipulation of numbers. At best, to predict how far a child may progress in those skills is difficult. The general approach to the use of numbers progresses from learning to identify, through counting and, finally, to the multiplication and division processes. Some of the major devices dealing with number symbols are *Race Horses* (C-2), *Thinking Caps* (C-43), *Counting Pans* (C-33), the *Ferris Wheel* (C-34), *Number Identification* (C-24), *Going to Town*

(C-15), *Number Casino* (C-36), *Dominoes with Pictures and/or Arabic Numbers* (C-35), *Over and Under* (B-33), *Clock Dial* (C-41), *Fantan* (C-37), *Number Columns* (C-40), and *Tone Counting* (B-31).

LETTER AND WORD IDENTIFICATION

In this section, which deals with letters, words and combinations of words, the same general vocabulary is used throughout. The emphasis, as far as recognition training goes, is on the basic 500 word vocabulary, which is generally sufficient for everyday elementary communication. Through the exercises employed here, the children learn to use the basic vocabulary with at least a minimum proficiency, to read the words with some facility and to write them to some degree. They identify words, match words, match words with objects and pictures, name objects, read printing and script, learn to print and write letters and words, and learn to spell words according to their similar sounds. The most important of these devices and techniques are *Opaque Projector* (C-25), *Hidden Objects* (B-17), *Counting Pans* (C-33), *Picture Word Books* (C-18), *Word Matching Cards* (C-19), *Word Racks* (C-20), *Writing* (C-32), *Sentence Building Frame* (C-21), *Spelling Blocks* (C-27), and *Story Telling* (C-22).

APPLIED GAMES

Many of the devices are frankly developed as games. These games may require a synthesis of prior training. However, many are also specific teaching and review techniques, independent of other devices. The general material with which the games mentioned here are principally concerned are word and number symbols. There are a few devices that deal with other perceptual concerns. The game devices that may be applied in this phase but apply more to the previous phase (initial perceptual training) are: *Masks and Bells* (B-28), and *Treasure Hunt* (B-32). Those game devices that apply more to this training phase are *Race Horses* (C-2), *Going to Town* (C-15), *Number Casino* (C-36), *Dominoes with Pictures and/or Arabic Numbers* (C-35), *Story Telling* (C-22), *Bark Splitting* (D-3), *Over and Under* (B-33), and *Fantan* (C-37).

CONCEPTUALIZATION

Though conceptualization may involve many sorts of mental activities, this activity consists essentially of the ordering, organizing and interrelating of objects and events in symbolic ways. We recognize it as an important and often necessary activity for reasonable or intelligent behavior. The more effectively an individual can deal with concepts, the more effective he can be in his overt behavior. To be able to form and to utilize concepts is important in making decisions, drawing conclusions, classifying and categorizing information, performing creative activities, etc. These abilities are developed in the use of such devices as *Walking Maze* (**D-17**), the *Mosaic Puzzles* (**B-18**), *Bark Splitting* (**D-3**), and *Number Columns* (**C-40**).

TRAINING EXTENSIONS

The activities considered here as training extensions are not the innovations of the Functional Teaching Program. However, it considers some of these exercises as necessary adjuncts to the pedceptual phase of the training program. We are referring here to such activities as instructional films, field trips, hiking, shopping, etc.

Chapter 7

MOTOR-PERCEPTUAL INTEGRATION

INTRODUCTION

IN THIS CHAPTER we are primarily concerned with activities that McGlone and others describe as manipulation, coordination, and integration. For the most part the exercises and the devices described here will be those that involve the coordination of motor activities with perceptual information.

The activities in this phase of training often require a combination of skills which were practiced in the preceding phases. However, now the tasks are often more complicated than before and in this fourth training period the child must continue to practice and to apply to new situations those perceptual and motor skills previously acquired.

In some respects, this phase of training can be related to Kephart's (24) description of the hierarchy of development of behavior patterns. That is, there are definite developmental states in the life of a child. Development in each stage normally depends upon and is related to development achieved in the prior stages of his life. Various motor exercises ordinarily occur early in the infant's life, with a consequent change or improvement in motor skill. Perceptual development then occurs, the nature of which is dependent not only upon sensory stimulation but also upon the preceding motor development. From then on, there develop more complicated cognitive-integrative activities. This chapter will consider that phase of training which involves devices and exercises that may facilitate the growth of cognitive or integrative skills.

An important aspect of this phase of training is the coordination of motor activities to various perceptual experiences. Such coordination will be discussed under topical subheadings in this chapter. It will be noted that since many of the requirements of human life are dependent upon the appropriate use of the hands and arms, this phase of training contains many exercises that contribute to the skillful use of these parts of the body in the manipulation of objects in coordination with perceptual information.

PERCEPTUAL-MOTOR INTERACTION

In this section the emphasis is placed upon exercises which clearly require an interaction between perception and motor behavior. Such interactions are often extremely complicated. Adequate motor behavior control is not only a serious problem itself but, in addition, every perception that we make in some way or another may have an influence upon our subsequent perceptions. Hence, the devices and exercises utilized in this stage of training can have important and complicated effects in expediting the growth and improvement of basic skills involved in the learning processes of mentally retarded people. Among the devices that deserve to be emphasized here are the *Slot Boxes* (**B-3**), *Discs on Nails* (**B-15**), *Jumping Peg ("Peggy")* (**C-3**), and *Shell Puppets* (**C-16**).

KINESTHESIS AND VISION

Here we are chiefly concerned with the coordination between distinctive visual cues and resultant motor activity. As we have mentioned, bringing about improvement in any particular muscular activity, as well as being important in its own right, may influence future motor development and facilitate the improvement of perceptual skills. In the daily life of a mentally retarded individual, as in the daily life of any individual, there are many activities, developments and improvements in which this cause-and-effect relationship is evident. That is, visual cues can determine the direction, strength, precision, the very nature of muscular activity. Very often in retarded children, particularly those in the lower IQ ranges, this coordination between visual cues or visual perception and motor activity is poorly developed and in some cases even nonexistent. Thus, according to the teaching rationale proposed in this book, such coordinations need to be emphasized. The devices listed below do not include every device that may aid the development of relationships between vision and motor activity but constitute a representative core sufficient to lead to a closer coordination of the child's visual perceptions to muscular activities. Let us mention here four devices that are specific to this aspect of training: *Wired Hose* (A-2), *Hoopla Ball* (C-28), *Sweeping Box* (D-1), and *Basket Weaving* (D-10). Other exercises are described in Part II.

TACTILE SENSE AND VISION

The primary concern here is with the joint effect of tactile cues and visual cues, so necessary to fine finger and hand movement and to coordination. Of course, this is related to the preceding section on motor activity and vision. It is implied here that upon touching an object and upon seeing an object, a relationship develops: the child learns to be able, by touching an object, to imagine what it looks like; or, on seeing something, to be able to anticipate or know what it would feel like were he to touch it. Now, to learn such relationships is not particularly easy for many mentally retarded children. What then is often required in this stage of training is to develop more effective utilization of tactile cues, which will require the child to attend more closely to his tactile sensations. Then, it is very important that he learn to relate these tactile sensations or perceptions to appropriate use of hands and fingers. Finally such tactile perceptions must, under many circumstances, be related to the visual perceptions which are coordinated. Of course, included in the tactile sense are not only pressure cues but also sensations of pain and temperature. Some exercises that are particularly relevant here are the *Companion Cube* (A-3), *Dressing Techniques* (B-24), *Bead Threading* (B-6), and *Bolt and Nut Board* (B-13).

PERCEPTUAL-HAND COORDINATION

It is of great importance that mentally retarded students acquire as much skill as possible in the use and coordination of their hands and arms. Activities which require the proper use of one's hands and arms vary from such simple things as picking up an object, to opening a door, to manipulating a lock, to putting together objects, and so on. Any person who is handicapped in his ability to manipulate objects with his hands is, of course, at a great disadvantage. Since mental retardates often show great clumsiness in the use of their hands, it is very important to provide training which will develop more appropriate and improved use of whatever hand motor skills they may possess. A large number of the Laradon Hall exercises contribute to such an increase in the skill with which a child uses his arms and hands. Judging and maintaining appropriate tautness, in weaving activities for example, requires what is referred to as *muscle memory*. We can mention here just a few of the exercises that are particularly designed to increase these hand manipulation skills. There are **Knot Tying and Knot Untying** (**B-23**), the **Stringing Frame** (**"Birthday Cake")** (**B-7**), **Electric Maze** (**C-6**), the **Pattern Column** (**C-4**), and **Table Shuffleboard** (**C-39**).

PRE-ACADEMIC COORDINATIVE EXERCISES

All the exercises mentioned so far, as well as many others, often have effects in addition to those for which they are specifically designed. That is, certain devices concerned primarily with increasing a child's hand skills are so constructed that they may help him to learn colors, or shapes, or numbers, etc. They often contain important incidental cues with which the child may become increasingly familiar. In the Functional Program an attempt is made to design all devices in such a manner that each one may be used to help teach not only a specific subject in one particular way but, rather, to permit them to be used to achieve several objectives and to be used in different ways.

The following are particularly good examples of devices that contain these pre-academic types of coordinative exercises. There are **Writing** (**C-32**), **Bead Threading** (**B-6**), **Jumping Peg** (**"Peggy"** (**C-3**)**, and **Table Shuffleboard** (**C-39**).

COORDINATIVE GAMES

Games are invented and used for several reasons. Often, learning within the context of a game is a more pleasant way of learning. Frequently, one must work with a child who has a short attention span, low level of motivation, and a low tolerance level for the usual teaching methods. Also, many games give new opportunity to apply what has been previously learned in a somewhat different situation. Let us mention here some of the activities which are often so pleasing to the child that they can be referred to as games: *Jumping Peg ("Peggy")* (**C-3**), *Shell Puppets* (**C-16**), *Table Shuffleboard* (**C-39**), *Fling-A-Ring* (**D-11**), and *Miniature Maze* (**C-5**). Of course, many games not described here are within the capacity of developmentally retarded children.

PRACTICAL EXERCISES

There are many activities in the training program that are very practical in nature. Some of these exercises require actions that the child has to do for himself everyday; some are activities which he may be required to do in his work; some may contribute to the development of skills which he needs to take care of his personal needs; and some may contribute to skills which he may use in a sheltered workshop. All of these exercises contribute in some way to the development and improvement of coordination and manipulation. Particularly pertinent devices which can be mentioned here are *Shoe Lacing* (**B-25**), *Dressing Techniques* (**B-24**), *Knot Tying and Knot Untying* (**B-23**), *Sweeping Box* (**D-1**), *Fabric Weaving* (**D-9**), *Spool Knitting* (**D-8**), and *Basket Weaving* (**D-10**).

TRAINING EXTENSIONS

Some of the exercises mentioned in the preceding section are comparable to or are preparation for work which these children may be able to do in a sheltered workshop for mentally retarded people. Indeed, some of the activities are identical to those activities going on in the workshop at Laradon Hall.

Laradon Hall obtains contracts from various companies and agencies. These contracts involve manufacturing devices, assembling objects, packaging material, weighing and packaging nails, making candles, assembling rock specimens, painting small objects, gluing materials on cards, etc. In other words, the sheltered workshop may take on a variety of contracts involving activities which mentally retarded people can be taught to perform adequately. However, for the more severely retarded, various jigs, tools, techniques and procedures have had to be devised to enable the student to perform some of the more complicated functions which, because of his defect, he would not otherwise be able to perform. Never, in the performance of these job activities, is there concern only with production and the meeting of a contract. Rather, these workshop activities are intended to contribute also to further motor-perceptual development. In addition, they are intended to aid the trainee to acquire some values, to learn to work conscientiously, to cooperate, to become responsible, and to experience achievement and some feeling of worthwhileness.

Industrial class (sheltered workshop).

Let us describe some of these activities in detail. For instance, attaching strings to tags is a job which has been contracted to the workshop for some time. Since the first retardates to be trained for the work were not able to push the strings readily through the small hole in the tag, a crochet hook-like device was set in a heavy base. The trainee could, after attaching the string loop to the hook, pull up one of the tags, which had been placed on the rod of the crochet hook. Once the tag has been drawn up far enough so that the looped string was well within the tag hole, the trainee could then draw one end of the looped string through the other end of the loop, completing the operation. Since, at the inception of the contract, none of the workers could accurately count twenty-five stringed tags, and since the contract called for twenty-five stringed tags to be packed per box, a rack was designed which had twenty-five slots. When each slot in the rack was filled with a tag, then the bundle was an appropriate number. Now, since the string loops would become tangled up in the process of bundling, and the students took too long to untangle the disorder, an additional procedure was developed. A way was devised to put the string loops onto a frame, with a rubber hose as a holder, so that the worker could grasp one loop of string per time in an orderly fashion, thereby avoiding the tangle.

This entire job is quite complicated, but the task has been broken down into six relatively simple operations, each of which can be learned and performed efficiently by even rather severely retarded individuals.

The nail packaging project resembles an assembly line. The contract requires that nails of various sizes be packaged in one-pound lots, each lot to be placed in an appropriately labeled small cardboard box. In the beginning, weighing the nails in these one-pound lots proved to be the most difficult part of the job. Since the severely retarded trainees could not be depended upon to weigh the nails properly on a scale, a device was developed to get around this difficulty. One-pound lots of each sized nail was weighed out and counted. Then, for each type of nail a wooden disc was prepared. Into it were drilled holes of a size to accommodate the type of nail and in sufficient number to be filled by exactly one pound of that type of nail. Now, the worker has only to fill each hole in the disc with a nail and pass the disc to the next worker who inverts the contents into a circular pan. After a gentle shake to align the nails, the next worker takes them and places them in the cardboard carton. (The cartons themselves are prepared by other workers in the shop.) Finally, one of the trainees closes the carton and places it in a larger cardboard box.

From time to time the trainees switch about in their jobs. In this way, each of them profits from a variety of experiences in manipulating objects, assembling objects, packaging objects, pouring from one container into another and moving objects from one place to another. There are perceptual, hand-motor, coordinative activities required here which would have been impossible for these workers had the task not been broken down into simplified sections. With such a pattern many tasks normally limited to non-retarded individuals can be set up for retardates.

CONCLUSION

While we are describing an educational and training program, there are occupational aspects which cannot be separated from it. It is evident that the skills acquired in these operations, which are an integral part of the instructional program, have also obvious occupational significance.

Chapter 8

CASE HISTORIES OF INDIVIDUALS ENROLLED IN THE FUNCTIONAL TEACHING PROGRAM

INTRODUCTION

THE FOLLOWING are histories of persons who have been benefited by the teaching program described in this text. Although
concise and confined for the most part to essential data, they do
present, we hope, an understandable picture of what has been
done with each person, and what has been achieved.

The persons referred to here are all mentally retarded, with
IQ's ranging from 25 to 50. Their chronological ages range from
fifteen to forty years; some are day students, some are resident
students; both the causes and the degree of retardation in these
people differ; some show great retardation, some show no emotional disorder or physical handicaps. None of these individuals
had met the minimum prerequisites for attending the classes for
so-called *educables* either at Laradon Hall or in the public
schools, nor were they qualified for training in the occupational
center connected with Laradon Hall. They were considered to
be, at best, trainable, and at worst, custodial cases.

The five cases reported there, we believe, are typical with regard to the problems involved and the results attained. For the
benefit of the reader who may be interested in the detailed
manner in which the program meets the needs of the retarded
child the first case is related with careful attention to detail. The
subsequent cases are more concisely described with the intention
of providing at least a general impression to the reader.

Case 1

N. was born of parents who were both over forty years of age.
There were also in the family two sisters, one four, the other five
years older than N. The father, who had two years of college education, was employed by the state. The mother had a high school edu-

cation plus three years of nurse's training. N. was born one month prematurely but delivery, aided with an anesthetic, was normal. At birth the infant weighed four and one-half pounds and had one malformed toe, but seemed healthy.

It was not until five months after birth that an examination revealed mongoloid features of eyes, mouth and hands.

N.'s physical and psychological development was slow: she walked at three, talked a few words at four, was not toilet trained until she was five years old. The parents, realistic about the child's future, probably did as good a job as possible in raising N. It is scarcely remarkable that N., being the youngest member of the family in addition to being handicapped, was somewhat spoiled by parents and sisters.

When N. was five years old her father became afflicted with a heart disorder. The family moved to a large city where the father worked as a self-employed cabinet maker in a workshop attached to the home. Thus he could "keep an eye" on N. while the sisters were in school and the mother at her job as a public health nurse. A grandmother also moved into the home.

N. contracted no serious childhood diseases. In a medical and psychological report made when she was six years old N. is described as mongoloid, with development less than normal but to some degree higher than usual in mongoloids. This report mentions that N. did not know colors, could not complete the test on the form board, and had a short span of concentration. For several years after this report was made, N.'s parents continued her training at home. When N. was ten years old, the parents tried to enroll the child in a special class at one of the public schools. She was regarded as unacceptable because of her IQ of 36, her difficulty in remembering simple verbal rote material and because of her generally poor memory. Her ability to identify familiar objects was poor, her vocabulary quite limited, and she had difficulty in understanding simple requests.

Their search for a program or school in which their daughter could obtain more adequate training than they were able to provide at home finally led N.'s parents to Laradon Hall, where she was accepted as a day student. Psychological examination prior to admission revealed an IQ of 38 on the Merrill-Palmer Test; coordination and perception of form were good but the attention span appeared to be remarkably short. No obvious negative behavior nor acute behavioral problems, aside from the retardation, were apparent. During the following four and one-half years, the girl attended classes for trainable children and received individual speech therapy at Laradon Hall. At the end of this period, N. had acquired a relatively large vocabulary and could converse willingly and meaningfully on many subjects. However, articulation was sloppy and there were frequent distortions, presumably due to her large and very sluggish tongue and the rapidity of her speech. Her progress in class and speech therapy was steady but slow.

In the summer of her fourteenth birthday, N.'s father died suddenly. A psychological examination in the same month revealed that apparently the death had had no marked influence on the child, and N. was cooperative as ever. However, a few months later there were reported signs of stubbornness, compulsiveness, demandingness and of a reduced ability to share with others. Her IQ on the Merrill-Palmer test then was 39, about the same as three years earlier. This was an astonishing fact, as the IQ of mongoloids supposedly decreases from the eleventh year on. Her motor performances were good, her perceptual skills were weak, and there was little sign of concept formation.

Since N. was adjusting well at Laradon Hall, the mother decided to continue the enrollment. No change was observed in N.'s performance or behavior during the remainder of the year.

The following fall, though her warm relations at home with mother, sisters and grandmother did not change, a teacher noted that at school she was becoming bossy toward her classmates, teasing and harassing the younger ones. At the same time her interest in classwork lessened, her academic performance declined and came, in some cases, to a standstill. As N.'s continuation in her class did not promise behavioral and academic improvement, she was transferred to the Industrial Class and workshop.

Although N. had no particular motor difficulties, she did have a major problem in her inability to sustain attention on any task. With the help of generous praise and admonition, this problem was to a great extent resolved. Her assignments were changed often, lest her distraction be "aimlessly moved." She worked a great deal with devices which are intended to widen and intensify general perceptual awareness, such as **Hidden Objects (B-17), *Mosaic Puzzles* (B-18), *Walking Maze* (D-17), *Pattern Column* (C-4), *Over and Under* (B-33), *Weight Watching* (B-11), *Sound Matching* (B-29), *Fantan* (C-37), *Skull Pairing* (B-16),** and **Odors (Bottled Odors) (B-2).** In this way, N. was given the opportunity to experience a wide range of impressions involving the different sensory stimuli—visual, auditory, olfactory, tactile, and kinesthetic.

Since she showed poor ability in differentiation, the next step was devoted to developing the ability to perceive differences and similarities as well as to the improvement of her memory. To achieve these ends, N. passed all stages of *Separation of Objects (B-4* and *B-5)* and practiced on the devices **Colored Yarns (B-8), Colored Nail Board (C-17), Colored Cubes (B-14), Long and Short (B-12), Colored Yarns,**

Shaded (**B-9**), *Inset Puzzles* (**B-10**), etc. When it became apparent that N.'s memory and sensory functions were improved, attention was focused on what was probably her greatest need: the coordination and integration of various sensory impressions. With practice on such exercises as *Pattern Matching (C-8, C-9, C-10, C-11 C-12* and *C-13)* in all its variations), *Triple Card Matching* (**C-14**), *Writing* (**C-32**), and *Picture Word Book* (**C-18**), definite progress was soon being made on "practical" experiences such as *Bolt and Nut Board* (**B-13**), *Discs on Nails* (**B-15**), *Bead Threading* (**B-6**), *Spool Knitting* (**D-8**), and others. In addition, N. also learned fabric and basket weaving.

Hand-in-hand with the apparent improvement in perceptual activities, demonstrated by her mastery of the various procedures mentioned, there occurred a striking widening of N.'s vocabulary. In view of this latter development an attempt was made to develop reading and writing skills. Contrivances such as *Word Matching Cards* (**C-19**), *Word Racks* (**C-20**), *Sentence Building Frame* (**C-21**), *Spelling Racks* (**C-27**), *Story Telling* (**C-22**), and others were now employed as was *Word Development* (**C-29**).

Progress in reading and writing was steady but slow. (The probable reasons for this will be discussed later in the case history.) N.'s ability to count improved rapidly; the problems presented by *Dominoes with Pictures and/or Arabic Numbers* (**C-35**) *Clock Dial* (**C-41**), *Counting Pans* (**C-33**), and *Arithmetic Problem Boards* (**C-7**) were solved without undue difficulty; and she soon acquired a workable knowledge of numbers up to fifty. Finally, N. could accurately add one, two and three number figures by operating the apparatus, *Number Columns* (**C-40**).

Now nineteen years of age, N. is a healthy, friendly, mannerly young lady. She is clean and neat in appearance, a real member of her group, socially at ease, sometimes a bit jealous of other girls, but within the limits of expected behavior for girls of her age. Her bossy attitude has almost completely disappeared. She is good humored most of the time, pliable, and helpful to other pupils. She enjoys all physical activities, especially roller skating, swimming and dancing. Her memory in general, as well as her ability to remember words, names of persons, dances, etc., has improved immensely. With accuracy and speed she accomplishes tasks with three or four variables after listening attentively to the given order. Though she is still easily distracted, her attention span, nevertheless, is considerably extended, especially when she is working on a definite assignment. Her work in the Industrial Workshop of the Functional Program (unskilled and semiskilled labor) places her as a financial asset to the workshop and she exhibits some sense of competitiveness and ambition. Although her articulation is not distinct, her speech is more intelligible than previously. The latest IQ score was 48 (WAIS) showing an increase of about ten points within nine years.

At home, where things generally run relatively smoothly, N. is cooperative, keeps everything tidy, and lends a hand where she can. She does not attempt to read at home, but looks at pictures in magazines and likes to watch T.V. Some of her behavior, such as the continued high susceptibility to distraction, her discomfort when looking at stationary objects for a longer time, and the habit of looking out of an angle of the eye, seems to betray a "visuo-autonomic defect" (see Gellner, 10) which may explain in part her relatively slow progress in reading and writing.

There is great affection between N. and her mother and the one sister still at home. The other sister has married and now has a child. Whenever N. is with the baby she is completely absorbed in its care, forgetting everything around her. She has pleasant interactive contact with the children of the neighborhood, loves the smaller ones and is—if not teased—a good companion to the older ones.

Case 2

J. was the first child of a twenty-seven-year-old mother. He was early recognized as mongoloid. Five years later a normal daughter was born. The father is a high-school graduate. He left the mother soon after the birth of the second child. The mother has three and one-half years of college training, works as a medical technologist, and lives with her father and daughter in a large city in Colorado.

J. did not start to walk until he was about twenty-six months of age. He apparently could not talk in even two to three word sentences before he was four years old. Childhood illnesses included measles and chicken pox. Temper tantrums were among his common behavior problems.

After attending, for one year, a special class in public school, he was dismissed because of severe mental deficiency. Another six months of private tutoring produced no remarkable results. A Merrill-Palmer Test administered during his thirteenth year revealed an IQ of 40 (MA five years).

When J. was fourteen years of age, he came to Laradon Hall. He could feed himself, dress and undress, wash and bathe himself and his toilet habits were satisfactory. He would eat only starchy foods, practically never would he digest meat, fish, fruit, vegetables, etc. A report issued in that same year indicated that his vocabulary and understanding of words was relatively good. His color perception apparently was normal. Auditory and visual abilities were fair. Eye and hand coordination were adequate. He adjusted rapidy to the social demands of the school and quickly acquired reasonable food habits.

A general report issued the following year indicated that J. had very little interest in reading, that he could count only by rote and lacked workable number concepts. The speech therapy probably led to an improvement in his vocabulary. A psychological report written at the end of the same year states: "J is a trainable child, but it is doubtful that he will ever be able to live in society without constant supervision." In a medical report of that time, J. is noted as being a "typical mongoloid with a mentality below IQ 50." In that same year (he was now seventeen years of age) J. was transferred to the Occupational Center of Laradon Hall. An evaluation report after eight-weeks training notes that J. was very poor on specific aptitudes related to visual-motor, kinesthetic and gross coordination, and that he also was poor in manual dexterity. He was average (for his chronological age and IQ level) in motor memory, above average in visual memory and good on verbal memory tests but did very poorly on an abstraction ability test. He had a picture vocabulary age of 5-5 (Peabody Picture Vocabulary Test), and did not recognize written numbers, although he could recite consecutive numbers correctly. On the job J. was a slow worker although very cooperative. As J. could not comply with the basic requirements of the Occupational Center he was assigned, after a year, to the Industrial Class and workshop of the functional program. After nineteen months of training there, another general report was made. Although the full Scale WAIS score revealed an IQ of not more than 48, J. had improved in several abilities and skills. His enunciation was clear, his vocabulary was in the range of five years (according to a Peabody Picture Vocabulary Test Form B.). J. seemed extraordinarily ambitious and would stick to his tasks even in spite of ordinarily disruptive distractions.

At the time of this writing J. is now much improved in understanding and in applying common sense in carrying out oral instructions. He can add three-number figures with the help of the Number Columns. He can write and read his name. Also he can read such signs as *danger, poison, entrance, exit, stop.*

He likes to look at pictures in magazines but is not fond of reading or watching television. Perhaps one reason is that he suffers from impairment of vision—despite glasses. The impairment may be related to a neurological involvement.

J. is a resident student, well-behaved, and does his chores in the dormitory satisfactorily.

Case 3

P. was the first child of a twenty-two-year-old mother. The father deserted the mother before the child's birth. The mother remarried a year after P.'s birth and has since had two normal male children. P.'s birth was difficult, labor extended over three days and delivery was aided with instruments. The infant was blue at birth and apparently lifeless until revived by the attending physician. Weight at birth was seven and one-half pounds. Head control developed at seven months, crawling at nine months, walking after ten months, talking a few single words at twelve months and short sentences after twenty-four months.

The first intelligence test score was obtained when P. was nine years of age. The IQ on the Stanford-Binet was estimated to be 31. The child was diagnosed as epileptic and severely defective mentally at that time. She was enrolled in Laradon Hall at the age of thirteen. Reports of a physical examination at this time note: a slight slump in left hip; left foot and left arm slower in growth, slow movement, poor coordination, waddling type of gait, and left hemiplegia. She had, in addition, suffered convulsions about every three months since the age of nine months, and had little comprehension of surroundings.

The next year, the WISC test showed an IQ of 31. Reports indicate that she was disinterested in the test, easily distracted and emotionally unstable. The summary statement of the tester: "I doubt if she can ever achieve anything intellectually. There is much emotional disturbance in addition to her organic handicap."

P. was in the regular instructional (nonfunctional) program at Laradon Hall for almost six years. Speech therapy was initiated early with some progress. A Stanford-Binet test again revealed an IQ of 31 at the age of sixteen. At this time she could print her name, had no evident number perception, was extremely poorly coordinated, and could not draw geometrical forms. Her attention was difficult to hold, she was shy, her speech slurred, and she appeared to distrust her abilities. The general impression of the examiner was that she would be capable of little more than routine activities under constant supervision. Reports from teachers a year later stated: memory span quite short, no sentence formation, reading and spelling skills little more mimicking the teacher. Progress was thought to be slight. General feeling at that time was that further academic progress and intellectual development should not be expected.

During her nineteenth year, P. worked for several months in the then newly established Occupational Center of Laradon Hall. Her performance there was reported to be at a very low level, attention span very short, manual dexterity and visual-motor coordination very poor, her behavior emotionally unstable. Later that year P. was enrolled on a trial basis in morning sessions in the Functional Industrial Class and continued to work in the Occupational Center during the afternoons. As this arrangement proved unsatisfactory, the next spring P.

joined the functional Industrial Class during mornings and the work-shop of the Industrial Class in the afternoon periods. Reports of examinations one year later (she was now twenty years of age) were rather encouraging. P. was said to be pleasant, cooperative, with no apparent behavior problems. She appeared to be contented, happy in her industrial training, which included work on subcontracts in the sheltered workshop where, eventually, she became outstanding in efficiency.

The latest psychological examination (she is twenty-three years of age at this writing) reveals significant improvement in memory and dexterity. Also, her discrimination of shapes and colors is good; she now perceives cause and effect relationship; reads printing and cursive writing of the simpler grade; draws with precision, has fair number perception and acts less impulsively. Her speech has vastly improved in respect to quality and substance and she is now able to work attentively up to three hours at a stretch.

Case 4

R.'s parents were healthy and R. was their first child. A sister, two years younger than R., died at five weeks from congenital heart disease. There is a normal brother, four years younger than R.

The father is a university professor; the mother holds an A.B. degree. The birth was premature at eight months gestation, but there were no reported complications. The child weighed 5 pounds, 15 ounces at birth.

The biological and physical development of the infant was slow: walking after seventeen months, talking a few single words at thirty months, toilet trained at four years. It is recorded that R. ceased talking or learning when he was less than two years old, about the death of an uncle and shortly thereafter the death of his baby sister. This reported transitory muteness (whatever its cause) lasted till he was four years old. He had a tonsillectomy at four and one-half, contracted measles at five, mumps at seven, virus pneumonia with a major convulsion at seven and one-half, chicken pox at eight, and infectious-mononucleosis at fifteen. Three months later, i.e. at about sixteen years of age, a second major convulsion occurred. From infancy he has been inclined to be very susceptible to motion sickness and to hay fever. His vision is limited and corrected by glasses. There is some spasticity. R. has been in special educational classes, in private schools, and has worked with tutors since he was five years old.

At the age of six his IQ was reported as being less than 50. Two years later it was recorded that he could write and do some simple arithmetic. A psychiatric report during his fifteenth year states a severe mental deficiency (Stanford-Binet test IQ of 44), a lowered convulsion threshold, a shortening of the left leg by a 2 cm, poor coordination, but no other suspicion of a cortical disturbance. A psychological examination of the same year mentions that several of R.'s characteristics may be defense mechanisms: e.g. continuous grinning, detached relationship to people, and stereotyped behavior. There is even the suggestion in the records that his poor coordination may be a defense mechanism!

When R. first came to Laradon Hall at the age of fifteen, he was reportedly very frightened and bewildered. However, according to these reports, before long he appeared to like his class work, although he needed continual reassurance. His social behavior became more and more detached. He did not enjoy teamwork or group activity. He finally was so withdrawn that he would not look at a person talking to him. He moved his lips very little when speaking. Speech therapy appeared to lead to improvement: he responded better, looked openly at the therapist and improved in articulation. His speech problem was considered basically a personality problem, produced by fear of expressing any opinion. His motivation for any action was extremely low.

After a year and a half, R. was transferred to the Occupational Center at Laradon Hall. Here he met the minimal relevant job requirements but his remarkable slowness made him unfit for anything but a very low level of productivity.

During his seventeenth year, R. was subjected to psycho-therapeutic treatment. The reports of the psychotherapist relate that R. was autistic, declined to communicate as much as possible, applied still the inappropriate and unceasing grinning as defense mechanism and had poor spontaneity and productivity. The response to treatment was poor.

Since his languor made it impossible to keep him at the Occupational Center, R. was admitted to the Industrial Class and workshop of the functional program at the age of eighteen. A general report, after eleven months in the program, read: "His 'neuro-equilibrium' is showing remarkable gains. The motor reflexes are sharper. His ability to read printing and cursive writing is excellent by expected standards. His swimming and skating have improved remarkably. His number perception is growing. With the aid of the 'Number Columns' he can add three-figure numbers. His detachment is greatly decreasing. He starts more conversations with teacher and pupils."

A psychometric evaluation was made at the same time. R scored at the 48 percentile on the Metropolitan Reading Test in contrast to 31 percentile two years earlier. In the reading section of the California Achievement Test, he accomplished a total reading grade placement of 2.1. It should be noted that two years before he had rated too low to be eligible to take the test. Still a year later the records indicate that he took a more active interest in people and activities. Although he was still lacking spontaneity, his efforts to express his feelings, while still rudimentary, were far better than two years previously.

At the present time, according to psychological information, R.'s free associations have changed from completely oral material to more objective and imaginative material suggesting that his psychic development has continued. He shows significant improvement in following verbal directions. His manual dexterity and motor activities, in general, appear to be advanced. He makes fewer errors, and accomplishes the tests more quickly. His perceptual discrimination is greatly improved. R. is able to work on occupational tasks which involve a series of steps without constant supervision and to achieve an adequate though slow production. His reading ability is steadily improving, he has acquired a good number understanding, he displays more self-confidence and a higher degree of alertness; he even understands simple jokes. His motor coordination along with his visual perception show further progress. His school report indicates that he often enjoys being with his group and participating in group dances and games.

Case 5

D. appears to be a healthy, stocky young man without apparent physical abnormalities. He is of Japanese origin. Age of mother at D.'s birth was twenty-five. Pregnancy was easy, full term, but delivery was via caesarean section. There are two sisters, three and eight years younger, both with good academic records in school.

Developmental data showed that D. could sit up at ten months, walk at fifteen months, was toilet trained at twelve months and talking in single words at twenty-five months. When he was a year old he barely survived a severe case of rheumatic fever and since that illness has suffered from convulsions. Mental retardation was diagnosed by the physician at the time of the illness.

The father has worked at various trades. The mother is a high school graduate. At the age of five, D. started kindergarten in the public school system where he was retained for a second year, apparently because his teacher felt that he was mentally retarded. Shortly after the two years of kindergarten, he came to Laradon Hall but was withdrawn after one year as the transportation problem could not be solved by the parents. Then after experiencing difficulty in regular classes of the public schools he was placed, at the age of thirteen, in a state training school.

When his family moved to California, he attended there a developmental class for three years. Apparently he enjoyed the structured academic and social activities at that school. The father died suddenly after an operation and the family moved back to Colorado. D. remained at home, helping with such household chores as making his bed, cleaning his room, washing the mother's car, sprinkling and cutting the lawn. He also aided his mother in her job of making leather purses by doing the lacing.

He is not interested in sports, perhaps because of difficulty in motor coordination. He seems to have a good relationship with his two younger sisters but easily becomes resentful when he feels that they are trying to dominate him. He expresses his aggressiveness, verbally, not physically. The relationship with the mother, a warm and understanding woman, is, as always, good.

The mother, after her husband's death, tried to assume the father's role along with her functions as mother. She has found this task extremely difficult, particularly since she has realized that D. needed daily discipline activity. At home, he required constant stimulation and supportive help in order to accomplish an assignment. The mother became more and more convinced that working in a group under supervision would offer a solution. She applied for placement of D. at the Occupational Center of Laradon Hall when D. was seventeen years of age.

A psychological examination at that time revealed a Verbal IQ scale of 49, a Performance IQ scale of 67, a Full Scale IQ of 54 on the WAIS test. His general behavior was reported as being rather immature for his eighteen years, his cooperation was good, but his communicative ability was severely impaired. His thoughts were presented in a very loosely integrated, disorganized manner; he was highly distractible and his attention span extremely short. All tasks in the test were hurriedly completed with apparently little or no interest in results. He was very concerned as to how long the tests would last and he tired considerably during the testing session. On the verbal scale of the WAIS test he failed to make any points on the arithmetic and similarities tests, which may suggest impaired reasoning and lack of conceptual thinking. A low score on the digit span test, with a complete failure on the digits backwards portion, reflected memory deficiency. His responses on the Bender Visual Motor-Gestalt test and the Rorschach test were indicative of organic dysfunction, which is hardly surprising.

D. appeared to be noticeably weak in dealing effectively with reality. This weakness, coupled with academic and organic limitations, seemed to be a constant source of frustration. His behavior betrayed a feeling of inadequacy and futility as well as a poorly developed self-concept. His defense mechanism consisted primarily of perserverance, denial, withdrawal, and aggression. Some cultural deprivation was obvious.

A further report at the time of D.'s application to the sheltered workshop noted that he was quite active and was very inquisitive, asking numerous questions about the ongoing procedure. He could not provide accurate information about himself. The interviewer found it questionable whether D. should be a candidate for placement in the Occupational Center of Laradon Hall. It finally was decided to take him through the usual eight-week evaluation program in order to determine better his vocational training potential.

Later that year, the Occupational Center issued its first evaluation on D.: "He had a positive attitude towards others in his social behavior, yet poor communication abilities. His conversation was confined to superficial themes with constant repetitions. He reacted swiftly to ridicule and was deeply depressed when reprimanded. Though he appeared to be alert, he was yet very distractible with a negative attention span. Concerning practical skills, he could not phone nor tell time, had a poor number sequence, primitive coin handling, no ability for independent shopping. His motivation on the job was poor, being erratic, and often his behavior seemed to be aimed at attention-getting. He demanded constant supervision and often responded inappropriately to instructions. His memory was good in visual and poor in verbal-motor modality. His speech was rapid and slurred, his dexterity was remarkably poor, his discrimination, however, was adequate on simple material only, and poor on complicated and complex material. He showed potentiality on perceptual integration, but was lacking in higher logical ability." As a result of this report, it was decided to let D. spend a half day in the Industrial Class of the functional program and a half day in the Occupational Center.

An evaluation three months later, during his eighteenth year, stated that D.'s efficiency in the vocational assignments during the afternoon hours at the Occupational Center had doubled, his attention span widened, finger dexterity and eye-motor coordination greatly improved. D. responded better to motivation and showed some pride in work well done.

At the present writing, a year later, D. is still a half-day student in the Industrial Class where emphasis is placed on the improvement of his skills in simple arithmetic, reading, and writing. He shows interest, is ambitious about his progress, and enjoys being successful in his training program.

Case 6

When K. entered Laradon Hall as a resident student, he was seventeen years of age, the youngest of seven children and the only one living with the parents.

The father who operated a small farm was suffering from arthritis and a heart condition. The mother, also of poor health through diabetes, high blood pressure, and kidney ailment, cared for the household as well as she could. K. did some limited work on the farm.

K.'s mother was thirty-eight years old when he was born. She reported nausea and vomiting during the first four months of pregnancy which was full-term. The delivery was normal. K.'s neonatal period was complicated by hypoclycemia, a weight loss, lethargy, and poor respiratory functioning. Medical examination at fifteen months revealed delayed general development. At about this time, K. had surgery to close an opening in the throat. He fell from a tractor at age three. An EEG at age seven was abnormal, but an EEG at age fifteen showed no abnormality. K. was in general good health at the time of admission to Laradon Hall. The intake diagnosis indicated brain damage with moderate retardation. (The full Wechsler IQ was 48.) K. had attended a class for trainable students at a public school in a nearby community for six years, starting at age eight. However, he was terminated because his age of fifteen years was not compatible with that of the much younger students in class. Subsequently, he lived at his parents' farm. The parents felt that the isolation of farm life was detrimental to him; he often times appeared very lonely. They therefore applied for residential placement at Laradon Hall through the local welfare department.

The school reports indicated that K. had a short attention span, was easily distractible, could not work without supervision and became aggressive when teased by the other students. The intake testing confirmed moderate retardation with symptoms of confusion and anxiety. K. could read and write a few words, lacked any arithmetic skills and displayed wide gaps in the visual-perceptual area concerning shape, size, and position. In the motor area, his equilibrium was deficient, hypertonicity was obvious. On the other hand, his muscle tonus stamina, and spaital orientation were fair. His general attitude was insecure, but cooperative.

In order to remedy or offset his deficiencies, K. was placed in the intensive basic motor and sensory perceptual training of the Functional Teaching Program utilizing devices and methods described under A-7 through A-19 and Roller Skating (D-5), emphasizing exercises for gaining balance and body control. Work with Versatile Sticks (B-35), Pattern Matching (C-8 through C-14), and Colored Nail Board (C-17) appeared slowly but steadily to improve his visual-motor perception. With the aid of the Picture Word Books (C-18), his vocabulary was widened and his reading skills strengthened. In order to overcome his weak number knowledge, K. was introduced to the Problem Boards (C-7) combined with the use of Number Columns (C-40) and such games as Number Dominoes (C-35), Number Casino, (C-36), and Fan

Tan (C-35), etc. Recognizing his weakness in arithmetic, K. was initially afraid of number tasks and needed constant supervision and encouragement by the teacher to start and complete his tasks. A year later K. had to be asked to stop when doing number work.

Following placement in the Language Development Group there was marked improvement in his communicative skills. He was an attentive and cooperative participant in this group. With his improved eye-hand coordination, K. could create attractive items in the crafts class such as mosaic insets, paper flowers, bead necklaces, etc.

At the end of his second year at Laradon Hall, K. was transferred to the Industrial Class for an intensive prevocational training. Here, he did so well that he became eligible to enter the Occupational Program as a resident trainee, where he is receiving training for placement in a competitive job within the community.

Case 7

J. came to Laradon Hall as a twelve-year-old developmentally disabled, legally blind child. He had sufficient functional vision to allow him—with the aid of corrective lenses—to participate in the Functional Teaching Program.

J.'s medical history revealed that during the first year of life, he was treated for urinary difficulties and had renal surgery. His mental retardation and visual impairment were not diagnosed before J. was five years of age.

The boy lived at home with his mother and four other siblings, two of whom were older and two younger than J. He had entered special education classes in public schools at the age of six and remained there till admitted to Laradon Hall.

When J. was ten years of age, his father died of an acute cardiac condition causing for J. an increasingly difficult behavior problem with his family, particularly with a brother one year younger than J. For this reason, J. was referred to residential care at Laradon Hall, when the mother felt she was neglecting the other children, especially the younger ones, while attending to J.'s problems. Even J. expressed the feeling that he had to leave in order to avoid constant and increasing friction.

Test findings at intake revealed moderate retardation (full Scale Wisc IQ 50), very concrete thinking patterns, and significant limitations in all cognitive areas. His social judgment was weak. He displayed sufficient reading and writing skills to be used to as a means of written communications. His arithmetic skills were confined to simple addition. In the beginning, it was difficult for J. to be quiet in class and to listen to assignments and explanations of the teacher. His attention span proved to be short; however, when he was interested, as in crafts, he was a persistent student who did neat and accurate work with little supervision.

Visual-perceptual skills such as matching cards and working with puzzles, appeared relatively good. Numbers were a problem, especially with subtraction and telling time. His physical development was apparently arrested as could be expected from his visual impairment. Yet, his muscle tonus was good, also his motivation to participate in physical activities.

Using the Writing Exercises I (C-32-A), II (C-32-B), and III (C-33-C) and techniques described in (C-45), J. improved relatively quickly in his letter formation and spacing of words in printing. The Picture Word Books (C-18), Word Racks (C-20), seemed to increase his ability in spelling; he also made some gains in phonetic spelling.

With the help of the Number Columns (C-40), he was able to demonstrate, with Arithmetic Problem Boards (C-7), improved number knowledge so that he could proceed to comparisons, money concepts. single measurements, and other upper first grade skills.

His proficiency in crafts increased remarkably as, for instance, in cutting, clay modeling, weaving etc. He still had some difficulty with fine motor activities.

At the end of one year at Laradon Hall J. achieved a second grade level in arithmetic, his spelling vocabulary had greatly increased, his printing was very legible with his general attention span much extended.

With respect to the perceptual and basic motor area, there was good progress in eye-hand coordination and figure-ground perception and much improvement in balance, laterality, and spatial orientation—remarkable results considering his visual handicap.

At the time of this writing, J. is in his third year in the Functional Teaching Program. He displays good coordination, equlibrium, grace in advanced physical activities such as on the trampoline and tumbling mats. He performs very well in Roller Skating (D-5), both backward and forward, and can jump with his skates over a board six inches high. He dances well in square and circle dancing (D-4).

Academically, J. is reading on a third grade level with good comprehension. His letters and numbers are correct in size and shape. His number concepts in addition and subtraction are satisfactorily developed and his skills in multiplication and division are improving. In self-care, J. takes good care of his clothing, property, and grooming. Precommunity skills such as self-identity, telling time, using the telephone, obeying traffic signs, recognizing coins and their value are adequate. J.'s social behavior toward peers and staff can be called excellent. The same can be said for his behavior toward his mother and siblings when he is at home on weekends.

Generally, J. appears content and even-tempered. He is cooperative, sharing, and friendly; a willing, ambitious, and independent student, who will be a promising candidate for the Occupational Program within one and a half years when he reaches the required age of sixteen years.

PART II
AREAS OF INSTRUCTION

INTRODUCTION

T HE MATERIAL WHICH constitutes Part II of this book is presented as an example of a program guide in functional teaching. Like any guide of this type it is intended to be a part of a dynamic program; constantly being added to as new observations give rise to new teaching ideas.

The activities and devices described here are examples of some of those actually used in Functional Teaching.

Further descriptions of some of these may be found in the Appendix.

BASIC PHYSICAL-PERCEPTUAL
DEVELOPMENT

Units of Instruction

THE FIRST STAGE OF THE functional teaching program (for convenience designated by letter A) deals primarily with motor activity. Those mentally retarded children who do little to initiate their own motor activity need to be stimulated into doing so. The units described here are designed specifically to create the conditions and provide the stimulation which will initiate activity. Most of the exercises are intended to improve such motor functions as locomotion, body adjustment and maintaining balance. Further, the intent here is to help the child become more aware of his body and what it can do. In addition, some of the exercises may have the effect of impressing upon the child the nature of cause and effect relationships—those existing between himself and his environment.

This stage correlates roughly with the discussion in Chapter 4. The term *physical-perceptual* used in Part II also corresponds roughly to the term *motor-perceptual* utilized in Part I. The use here is, to a certain extent, arbitrary. *Physical-perceptual* is employed in an effort to better describe the specific nature of the activities presented. The activities are largely physical (in the sense of physical education) and the literature on which the discussion of the terms *perceptual* and *motor* is based suggests that physical (or motor) development in the infant precedes the perceptual. In order to express the evolvement of the term *physical-perceptual* in functional teaching and at the same time preserve the association with variations of *perceptual-motor,* both sets of terms are used in this book and may, in most cases, be used interchangeably.

For those interested in programming a brief example of a sequential lesson plan may be found in the Appendix.

A.1 *Feathers and Honey*

OBJECTIVES
1. To develop sensory awareness through tactile stimulation.
2. To develop manual skills.
3. To develop visual and motor coordination.
4. To further the development of the child's attention span.

MATERIALS
A drop of honey or syrup, supply of fluffy feathers (of different colors if possible).

SUBJECT MATTER
Sensory awareness through tactile stimulation.

PROCEDURE
Place thin film of honey on finger-tips of child and give him a supply of feathers which he will desire to remove. This activity should be continued over an extended period of time, as long as visual and tactile acuity need to be developed. Discontinue if the child appears frustrated.

A-2. *Wired Hose*

OBJECTIVES
1. To promote action and response on the part of the child.
2. To develop manual skills in the child.
3. To arouse the child's curiosity.
4. To stimulate continued action and the ability to attend.

MATERIALS
A rubber hose 2' long x $\frac{5}{8}$" diameter, corked on each end, and containing 3 lengths of flexible wire.

SUBJECT MATTER
Manipulation and coordination.

PROCEDURE
The child tries to bend the hose, causing it to jump into unusual positions. Encourage the child to try to control it and to note its movements.

A-3. *Companion Cube*

OBJECTIVES

1. To gain efficiency in finger manipulation.
2. To utilize the child's fingering habits.
3. To stimulate the child's curiosity.
4. To improve the child's ability to attend.
5. To promote recreational interests.

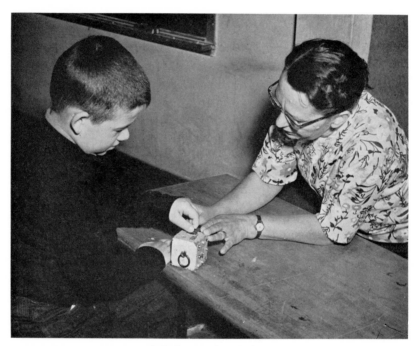

A-3. Companion Cube.

MATERIALS

A 4" wooden cube. On one face are several shallow holes into which the child can put his fingers. On another side are twenty-five raised nail heads in rows of five each way, equally spaced. On the third face is an iron ring, 1½" in diameter which turns, and can swing in all directions. The fourth face has on it a number of colored washers that are loosely attached by a single screw. On the same face, here are also two hinges, one opens from the top to the bottom, while the other opens like a door. Another side of the cube is covered with soft foam rubber, and the sixth face with coarse garnet cloth.

SUBJECT MATTER
Recognition of tactile and visual qualities through manipulation.

PROCEDURE
Hook the child's index finger through the ring and allow him to discover the interesting and different qualities of the cube.

A-4. *Chasing Mirror Reflections*

OBJECTIVES
1. To awaken response to visual stimuli.
2. To develop the child's ability to note visual and kinesthetic sensations.
3. To encourage the child to respond motorically.
4. To encourage physical movement.

MATERIALS
Flashlight in a dark room, or a mirror reflecting sunlight.

SUBJECT MATTER
Response to visual and kinesthetic sensations.

PROCEDURE
At first the teacher flashes the beam of light on the ground or a wall to stimulate the child's interest in following the spot of light. After the child observes reflected or beamed light and touches it, the teacher may change its position. This is continued until the child loses interest.

A-5. *Crawling Maze*

OBJECTIVES
1. To develop the child's kinesthetic responses.
2. To encourage the child to note variations in his own voice.
3. To aid the child to note spatial relationships with respect to his own body.
4. To aid the child to develop depth perception.

5. To provide opportunity to apply knowledge of numbers concepts.
6. To reduce fear of somewhat obscure places.

MATERIALS

Two parallel (lengthwise) tunnels with one inter-connecting space. There are 2 additional openings on one side. All openings are numbered. The apparatus may be made of bricks, lumber, concrete blocks or cement. The over-all dimensions are 5' x 4' x 18" high. On top of the Crawling Maze sand and dirt boxes may be built. (See illustration for B-1 Sand and Dirt Boxes).

SUBJECT MATTER

Body orientation, number knowledge, number recognition.

PROCEDURE

The child is encouraged to crawl through the tunnels. Next, he is given various problems which involve crawling into one tunnel and out of another specific one (the exits are numbered). When he is inside the tunnel he may be instructed to sing or call out in order to acquaint him with the different sounds of his own voice in a tunnel. Two children may be requested to explore the tunnel simultaneously.

A-6. *Water Pump*

OBJECTIVES

1. To develop the child's curiosity and exploratory tendencies.
2. To aid the child to establish connection between something he does and something that happens as a result of what he does.
3. To increase scope and complexity of sensory stimulation.
4. To aid the child to note tactile, kinesthetic, visual and auditory sensations and sensational changes.

MATERIALS

An old fashioned kitchen hand pump, mounted on a shelter which houses a small drum for water. Piping and other accessories necessary for operation of the pump.

SUBJECT MATTER
Experience of cause and effect relationships.

PROCEDURE
The child "discovers" the pump, or he may see other children using it. Allow the child to find the handle, grasp it, and put it into action until water is forced from the spout. Allow the child to do this several times at the first encounter.

A-7. *Balance Beam (With Mirror)*

OBJECTIVES
1. To aid in the development of the sense of balance.
2. To aid the child to become aware of the need to rely on abstract perceptual cues.
3. To aid the child to utilize visual, kinesthetic and labyrinthine sensations to maintain body adjustment.
4. To develop an awareness of the physical self and the potentialities of body movement.

MATERIALS
The apparatus consists of two planks, 2" x 4" and 2" x 8", each 8' long, and a mirror. These planks are screwed together to form a T, and are supported at either end by a rectangular board 2'6" x 1'6" x 2" thick (see illustration). These end supports make it possible to turn the "T" to expose any one of the three widths for the pupil to walk on. A three-piece mirror is attached to a wall facing one end of the beam, allowing the pupil to observe his own movements.

SUBJECT MATTER
Balance, body adjustment.

PROCEDURE
At the beginning, the apparatus is set as to expose the 8" face for the child to walk on. He may perform various exercises; kneel down, arise and continue to the center, or walk directly to the center and turn. Later, he may walk with a cup of water in his hand, or a bean-bag on his head, or carrying a tablespoon with a potato in it.

When he becomes proficient on the 8" face, he goes through the same procedure on the 4" face, and eventually with the 2" edge uppermost. Finally, he walks on the balance beam, repeating the exercises in the same order of difficulty, while watching his feet in the mirror. He is not allowed to look down at his feet at this stage, but is taught to watch his foot movements in the mirror.

As a variation, the angle of the beam is slightly changed (with respect to the mirror) and pupil must allow for this change of direction and the corresponding change of reflection that he sees.

A-7. Balance Beam.

A-8. Table Swing.

A-8. *Table Swing*

OBJECTIVES

1. To aid in developing awareness of labyrinthine, kinesthetic and visual sensations.
2. To develop an awareness of bodily movements.
3. To aid the child in the development of adequate body adjustments.
4. To help the child to respond to natural changes in the state of equilibrium.
5. To increase the child's awareness of his ability to cause something to happen.

MATERIALS

The apparatus consists of a 10' horizontal bar suspended between two braced "A" frames 7' high, with legs 10' apart at base. Wire cables covered with rubber hose hang independently from the horizontal bar. From them are suspended rectangular platforms made of $\frac{3}{4}''$ plywood. These platforms are of different lengths and widths and hang at different levels. (See illustration).

SUBJECT MATTER

Body adjustment, group interdependence.

PROCEDURE

This device is used by several (four to six) children at a time. They stand and swing, or walk from platform to platform, as they wish. The movement of one child stimulates movements in other parts of the swing, requiring the other children to adjust their positions. The rubber hose material covering the cables has a tendency to turn in the child's grasp, causing additional unexpected movements, which in turn, require adjustments on the part of the child. A teacher should always supervise this activity.

A-9 *Sinking Tires*

OBJECTIVES

1. To develop the child's awareness of his kinesthetic and visual abilities.
2. To aid the child to become aware of and develop the bodily movements involved in regaining and maintaining equilibrium.
3. To aid in the development of an adequate body image.
4. To develop reassurance in activities involving locomotion.
5. Physical exercise.

MATERIALS

The apparatus consists of one set of twelve auto tires. The tires, spaced at 18" intervals, are sunk vertically in cement to their lower inner rims. The inner edges of the tires are trimmed and cut in varying degrees; this produces various degrees in resiliency. It is recommended that a fence or a rail be placed near one side of the tires (see picture).

SUBJECT MATTER

Balance, gross motor coordination.

A-9. Sinking Tires.

PROCEDURE

The child is placed on the first tire (a firm one) with the help of the teacher. He walks on the top of the tires, which sink, often to an unexpected degree. The child should place the whole foot flatly on the tire, rather than heel first, lest he bend the tire to the outside. The railing along the tires gives the child a hold.

Finally, the child may walk without assistance.

A-10. *Climbing Obstacle*

OBJECTIVES

1. To develop the child's kinesthetic, visual and tactile acuity.
2. To provide exercise for the deliberate motions that are planned and executed to solve an immediate problem.
3. To place the child in a position in which he must call upon his physical resources in order to respond successfully to the demands of a situation.

4. To aid the child to become aware of his body adjustment and his self-image.
5. To provide opportunities for perceptual-motor coordination.

A-10. Climbing Obstacle.

MATERIALS

The apparatus consists of 2 steel tubing "A" frames connected by a 10' steel tubing bar at the top. On one side, hanging from this top bar, and anchored to the legs of the "A" frames at either end is a coarse mesh made of steel cable. The openings of the mesh are about $3\frac{1}{2}$" x $3\frac{1}{2}$" with the exception of the final row on each side; here the openings are 7" high x $3\frac{1}{2}$." On the other side, similarly suspended and anchored, is steel chain fencing.

SUBJECT MATTER
Perceptual-motor coordination.
Bodily adjustment, spatial orientation.

PROCEDURE
The pupil learns to climb up the side with the chain fencing, then down the cable side. The teacher should supervise this activity, encouraging the pupil to use his fingers and toes as much as possible on the chain side, and helping him to learn where to step without looking at his feet when climbing down the cable side.

Later, as he gains confidence, the pupil may climb with little supervision, and go up one side, over the top, and down the other side.

A-11. *Swinging Tunnel*

OBJECTIVES
1. To develop the child's kinesthetic and tactile perceptions.
2. To develop perceptual-motor coordination.
3. To provide large muscle exercise.
4. To aid the child to become aware of his bodily adjustment and of his self-image.
5. To provide the child with opportunities to respond to a variety of situations without the aid of familiar scenes or surroundings.

MATERIALS
The apparatus consists of three oil drums (from which the ends have been removed) suspended horizontally in line, end to end, from the connecting bar at the top of the ***Climbing Obstacle*** (**A-10.**) They are suspended (inside the mesh) from springs which are, in turn, attached to cables. Because of the springs, the movements of the drums are random and unpredictable.

SUBJECT MATTER
Body orientation and adjustment.

A-11. Swinging Tunnel.

PROCEDURE

The child is encouraged to enter a barrel and crawl through it, and through the two other adjoining barrels. The barrels sway horizontally, laterally, and vertically so that the child has to continually change his orientation position. At first the teacher helps the child into and out of the barrels. Later, the pupil enters and leaves the barrels on his own.

A-12. *Horizontal Ladders*

OBJECTIVES

1. To stimulate the child's kinesthetic, tactile and visual sensory awareness.
2. To develop physical coordination.
3. To aid the child to make sequential, step-by-step solutions to problems.

4. To provide opportunities for physical exercise and recreational outlet.

MATERIALS
The horizontal ladder, made of iron piping, is similar to the typical gymnastic device used in Physical Education. The ladder is supported by four steel pipes in the cross bars. It is slanted: one end is 10' and the other 8' above the ground. In addition, the ladder is bent in a concave manner. There is also a low horizontal ladder installation, standing 5' high, for stunts.

SUBJECT MATTER
Sensory awareness through gross physical movement.

PROCEDURE
All pupils start by hanging from the high ladder, holding a rung in their hands, and move forward rung by rung. In the beginning, the child may just hang without movement, in order to reassure himself.

After the student is efficient in going down, from the 10' end to the 8' end of the ladder, he goes *up* the ladder. Finally, he goes both *down* and *up*, frontwards and backwards.

The low ladder is for stunting, which is not allowed on the high ladder. Strict supervision is advisable in use of both ladders.

A-13. *Thimble Box*

OBJECTIVES
1. To develop manual coordination.
2. To develop manual dexterity.
3. To aid in developing handedness (laterality) .

MATERIALS
Plastic or plexiglass cube of $4\frac{3}{4}$", open on one face (e.g., five-sided) . Each of the five faces contains holes for large and small fingers. The holes are arranged in different patterns for varied exercises.

SUBJECT MATTER
Manual dexterity.

PROCEDURE

1. General

   Faces 1 and 4 each have four holes, arranged in a row, for use in opposing the thumbs and fingers. The holes in the corners are to be filled while the box is in various positions, first with left and then right hand fingers.

   In face 5 are large holes. Approaching the cube from the outside and with palm up, the child inserts a designated finger into one of these holes through the cube, and out again of a specified hole in one of the remaining faces.

2. On outside of box:

   Place Thimble Box on table with face 5 up. Teacher holds box firmly in place and tells, by pointing with pencil, which finger she wants placed in each hole. Only at the beginning does she touch a finger, and only in extreme cases does she move the box for the pupil's convenience.

   When the three holes in circles on faces 1 and 4 are filled, there will be two fingers left over. These *left over* fingers are used in other holes, as the teacher indicates.

3. From the inside of box:

   Have child fill all of the holes on face 5 with left hand fingers and then change over to right hand fingers while he holds the box. Fill all three holes on faces 4 or 7.

   Fill any of the holes and have the child hold the corresponding fingers of the other hand upon them. Repeat all exercises with both right, then left hands.

A-14. *Stepping Ladder*

OBJECTIVES

1. To develop motor coordination.
2. To develop posture and balance through walking exercises.
3. For exercise in working and negotiating barriers.

MATERIALS

Heavy wooden ladder 17' long with sides 13" apart. Rungs are cylindrical and of hard wood, 12" apart. Each end is reinforced by a length of 2" horizontal pipe which is bolted to the ladder. The middle of these horizontal pipes at the two ends is threaded to

A-14. Stepping Ladder.

vertical pipes of same diameter, $27\frac{1}{2}''$ long, at right angles. These vertical pipes are drilled through at one inch intervals to hold cotter pins.

The vertical pipes fit into other vertical pipes that are set in concrete their full lengths of $27\frac{1}{2}''$, the tops flush with the ground.

This makes it possible to adjust the ladder, which is parallel to the ground, raising or lowering it by inserting cotter pins.

SUBJECT MATTER
Gross coordination, posture adjustment.

PROCEDURE
The child walks, placing his feet between the rungs of the ladder. Begin with ladder 3" off ground. Teach the child to place one foot before the other in turn and in separate, adjoining spaces. If necessary, tap the child's foot with a yardstick and point to the space where that foot should be placed. As skill grows, gradually raise ladder to height of knees or higher. Later, as a variation, the child can repeat the process walking backwards. At no time allow the child to hold ladder rails while walking.

A-15. *Suction Blocks (and Related Apparatus for Breath Control)*

OBJECTIVES
1. To aid the child to associate holding and control of breath with thought and movement.
2. To encourage response and adjustment to changes in the situation.
3. To develop breath control needed for producing good speech.
4. To aid the child to delicate coordinations while under stress.

MATERIALS
Box $5\frac{1}{4}$" wide, $8\frac{1}{4}$" long and $1\frac{1}{4}$" high. Tops and sides are cut through with holes slightly larger than the blocks that are to be blown or dropped through them. Six blocks of $\frac{3}{8}$" balsa wood cut into various shapes as shown in drawing.

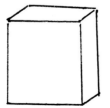 

Two discs, also of balsa. One disc is 1″ in diameter and $\frac{3}{8}$″ thick. The other is 1″ in diameter and $\frac{3}{4}$″ thick.

Table tennis balls. Colored fluff feathers. Box of tiny marsh-mallows. Fifty plastic soda straws or quills. Bottle of suitable antiseptic when quills are to be used more than once.

SUBJECT MATTER
Breath control.

PROCEDURE
Using quills, the blocks are picked up by suction and dropped into the appropriately shaped holes in top of the box.

Blocks are blown into the holes in the sides of the box, both lengthwise and sideways.

Still using quills, pupils blow one or more balls across table. With two or more playing, one pupil tries to blow his own colored feather across the table and onto the floor while others try to pre-vent action.

For suction, pupil draws a small piece of marshmallow against his quill and deposits it on a paper 6″ to 10″ away. Allow him to eat it as a reward.

A-16. *Tread Mill*

OBJECTIVES
1. To develop body coordination.
2. To provide for exercise and development of foot and leg muscles.
3. To aid in the development of balance and postural adjustment.

MATERIALS
Eleven rollers from washing machine wringers, 11″ long, set in hardwood 2″ x 4″ and 36″ long. The rollers are placed so that there is a difference of $\frac{3}{4}$ of an inch in height of alternating rollers. The hardwood rails are held 12″ apart by cleats at both ends. At one end, there are iron hooks in each rail.

Two uprights made of $1\frac{1}{4}$″ pipe, 42″ apart and are joined at the top by a cross pipe. Across the bottom are four cross rungs placed at 3″ intervals from the ground. By placing the hooks on the need of the rollers over one or another of these rungs, the incline (of the rollers) can be controlled.

SUBJECT MATTER
Gross coordination.

PROCEDURE
With plane hooked at lowest rung, have the child hold to bar upright, lean forward and push with his feet as he steps "on place." Raise plane as child gains skill. With shoes off do the same exercise. This exercises the arch.

A-17. *Spiral Drum*

OBJECTIVES
1. To awaken the child's responses to his environment.
2. To aid in the development of sound discrimination.
3. To aid the child to establish connection between something he does and something that happens as a result of what he does.
4. To help the child to discover his motor capabilities.

MATERIALS
Oil drum 29″ high and 19″ in diameter, hung horizontally 15″ above the ground between two by fours that are set in concrete. The only opening in the drum is in one end through which materials are passed for making different sounds, if desirable. Around the drum is painted a continuous spiral stripe, $\frac{1}{2}$″ wide, which makes four circuits from one end of the drum to the other.

SUBJECT MATTER
Experience of *cause and effect*.

PROCEDURE
The child discovers and explores the drum with no help or direction. He finds that he can revolve the drum and is amazed that he can cause the stripe to move across it.

A-18. *Seesaws*

A. Back-and-Forth Seesaw
B. Lateral Seesaw

OBJECTIVES
1. To stimulate the child to direct and control his body movements.
2. To develop balance and postural adjustment.
3. To develop directionality, positionality and laterality.
4. To develop a sense of rhythm.
5. To emphasize interaction in a group situation.

MATERIALS
Plank $7\frac{1}{2}''$ by 10' long bolted, 2" from each end, to auto tires that are set in concrete deep enough to cover the lowest portion of tire by 1". In the back-and-forth seesaw the tires are set crosswise to the length of the plank. In the lateral seesaw the tires, instead of being set crosswise, now run in the same direction as the board.

SUBJECT MATTER
Balance, rhythm.

PROCEDURE
A group of up to seven small children straddles the board and starts action back and forward or side to side. The teacher lends her strength only when necessary to keep the group in motion. The lateral plank sways because of alternate pushing of right and left legs combined with the rhythmic swaying of the bodies of the children. The forward and back plank moves when the children lean sharply and push back with their legs.

It should be noted that the equipment here used replaces the somewhat dangerous (especially for retarded children) traditional seesaw.

A-19. *Midget Teeter (Bongo Boards)*

OBJECTIVES
1. To develop balance and postural adjustment through "disequilibrilizing" exercises.
2. To aid the child to become aware of a sense of motor and rhythm.
3. To develop foot and leg coordination.
4. To develop laterality.

MATERIALS

Two 18″ long hardwood boards each bolted in the middle. Between them is loosely bolted a slotted $1\frac{3}{4}″$ pipe. The bottom board is, in turn, bolted to a concrete base. The top board acts as a miniature teeter board.

SUBJECT MATTER

Posture adjustment, balance.

PROCEDURE

The pupil stands on board, feet apart and across the length of board. He shifts his weight from left to right without having to step off board. He then does the same while facing the length of the board.

Later, still facing the length of the board, he shifts weight, turns on the balls of his feet and reverses his position. This action —back-to-front-to-back—is repeated several times with a slow, regular rhythm.

BASIC PHYSICAL-PERCEPTUAL SKILLS

Units of Instruction

THE CONCERN IN THE second stage of the functional teaching program deals with the child's needs to sense, to perceive his world. The exercises are designed to offer a wide variety of sensations and demand an increasing accuracy of perception. Recognition of stimulus similarities and differences is emphasized. The exercises require the use of visual, auditory, tactile, olfactory, and kinesthetic senses. This material corresponds roughly with the discussion in Chapter 5.

In contrast to stage A which deals with underlying functions or abilities, primarily physical ones having to do with gross body movements, the present stage is concerned with the introduction of specific outcomes, namely, skills. A word of explanation may be in order here. The literature of education and psychology recognizes a distinction between abilities and skills. Correspondingly, with functional teaching, Part I of this book deals more with the rationale behind general abilities which we hope to enhance and develop while Part II presents specifically that which we expect the child to gain from these activities.

B-1. *Sand and Dirt Boxes*

OBJECTIVES
1. To provide activities in which the children can experience various tactile sensations.
2. To provide activities which permit the child to manipulate objects and materials.
3. To develop the child's manipulative ability.
4. To provide opportunities for children to create through manipulation of objects and materials.
5. To provide for the child opportunities for noting similarities and differences, e.g. texture.

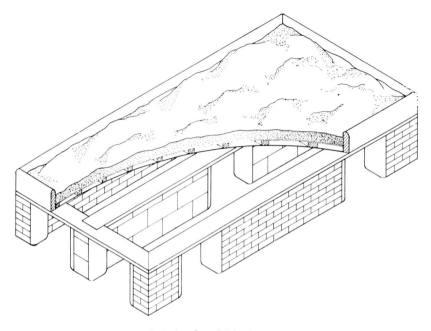

B-1. Sand and Dirt Boxes.

MATERIALS
1. Sand box, elevated 30″ above ground, equipped with plastic bottles, funnels, scoops, cans and coarse shakers.
2. Dirt box, elevated to 30″ above ground, with jello moulds, cake pans, spoons, trowels, flower pots and cookie cutters. Dirt in box is composed of garden loam, vermiculite, gypsum, a measure of fine sawdust and enough water to hold shape.

SUBJECT MATTER
Awareness of texture, form.

PROCEDURE
The children start playing at the sand box. Interest the pupils in seeing the sand flow from the bottles, funnels and scoops. In the dirt box the pupils are encouraged to mould objects. This requires keener manipulation and the ability to see form and mould the object. It also exercises the imagination.

B-2. *Odors (Bottled Odors)*

OBJECTIVES
1. To develop the utilization of olfactory senses.
2. To aid the child to discover similarities and differences through olfactory stimuli.
3. To aid in language stimulation.
4. To develop the ability to attend to a particular center of attention.
5. To aid in the development of breath control.

MATERIALS
Ten bottles, containing materials of different odors. Each bottle contains one of the following materials, each of which possess a distinctive scent:

1. Eucalyptus
2. Wintergreen
3. Vanilla
4. Camphor oil
5. Linseed
6. Pine oil
7. Clove
8. Onion
9. Garlic
10. Benzoin

SUBJECT MATTER
Sensory discrimination through olfactory sensations.

PROCEDURE
The pupil is presented with two distinct and different odors in succession. The teacher takes the lid off of the bottle and holds or passes it slowly beneath the student's nose, allowing him two or three inhalations. The name of the contents is pronounced distinctly by the teacher as the child smells, and he repeats the word as best he can. The next bottle is presented in the same manner. This procedure is followed with each pupil until all have had a turn. Then the other odors are presented.

When progress is shown, the teacher may use a single odor, asking each pupil in turn to name the odor. She also permits students to request certain odors, while following the rule that each child gives the name of each odor.

The tops of bottles should not be handled by the students. The children themselves may pass a bottle around after they have learned not to touch the bottle with the nose.

B-3. *Slot Boxes*

OBJECTIVES
1. To develop eye, arm and hand coordination.
2. To teach the child to recognize different shapes and colors.
3. To develop manual dexterity.
4. To aid in increasing the child's attention span.

B-3. Slot Boxes.

MATERIALS
1. Plain and colored spools; box with a hole large enough to admit spools; cards and strings.
2. One box on whose six sides is a differently colored spot, in the center of which is a hole of distinctive size and shape. Another box in which the first box fits, called "holder." Many wood

blocks, of shapes and colors to correspond to the holes and colors on the sides of the boxes.

SUBJECT MATTER

Discrimination of form.

PROCEDURE

For the Spool Box:
1. The child is encouraged to place the spools in a box which has a hole large enough to admit the spools. The aim is to have him do this on his own accord until all the spools are in the box.
2. Another activity is to encourage the child to thread the spools on a cord.
3. Another activity is to put the colored spools on a string.
    a. First, string the same colors together until all of them have been strung.
    b. Next, string them in a repeated color pattern (e.g., one blue, one white, and one red, then repeat). More complex patterns may be developed as the child gains efficiency.

For the Block Box:
The box is set in the "holder" so that only one face of the box at a time is exposed. The pupil puts into the opening all the blocks which are both shaped like the hole and colored like the spot. Then the box is turned to expose a different shaped hole, and the procedure is repeated. When the student is proficient, discard the holder, and the child will not find the hole that fits the block. When more proficient, let the child use the holder, but use uncolored blocks.

B-4. *Separation of Objects A* and
B-5. *Separation of Objects B*

OBJECTIVES
1. To develop the ability to identify objects.
2. To develop the ability to note similarities and differences.
3. To develop the ability to note location, shape, size and color in progressively more difficult lessons.

4. To aid in increasing the child's attention span.
5. To develop speed and accuracy in hand manipulation.
6. To encourage left to right movement.

MATERIALS

Several containers, each holding bracelet charms and other small objects, as:

1. Fish
2. Schooners
3. Washers
4. Bowling pins
5. Pistols

6. Monkeys
7. Fairies
8. Nuts
9. Screws
10. Several boxes of buttons, which vary in shape, color and size.

SUBJECT MATTER

Classifying objects.

PROCEDURE

Two containers, each holding a different sample are placed before the child, one to left, one to right. From a pile containing a variety of mixed-up objects, he selects an article to match the sample in the left-hand container, and deposits the selected object with its mate. He does the same for the container on the right. He repeats this left to right process until he has separated into proper containers all the matching objects. When ability warrants, other boxes and objects are added.

B-6. *Bead Threading* and

B-7. *Stringing Frame ("Birthday Cake")*

OBJECTIVES

1. To develop eye, finger, hand and arm (physical-perceptual) coordination.
2. To lengthen the child's attention span.
3. To develop finger dexterity.
4. To develop color sense.

MATERIALS

White spools (large) ; colored spools; assorted medium beads; assorted small beads; beading posts in a single circle (single

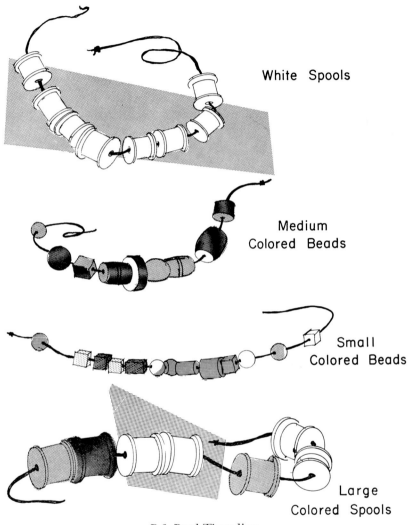

White Spools

Medium
Colored Beads

Small
Colored Beads

Large
Colored Spools

B-6. Bead Threading.

"Birthday Cake"); beading posts in a double circle (double "Birthday Cake"). (The posts on these devices have holes near the top and other holes at right angle near the center, to alternate the stringing of the posts. The double circle can be arranged to line up holes so that inner posts are opposite outer posts, or they can be staggered crosswise. The double can be used as two singles.)

SUBJECT MATTER
Discrimination of form, size, color, position and manual dexterity.

PROCEDURE
The child is introduced to the process of stringing, using large white spools on a large cord. As the child gains finger and hand dexterity along with eye coordination, gradually smaller spools of different colors, and finally, the beads are presented to him. He is encouraged to string the beads according to a pattern.

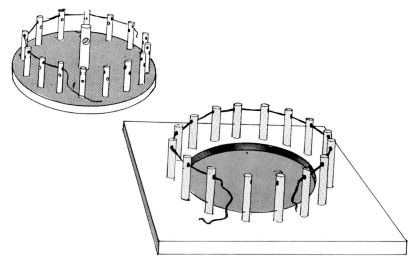

B-7. Stringing Frame ("Birthday Cake").

After he has gained efficiency in stringing on a cord, the single beading posts (called the "Single Birthday Cake") are introduced. This device compels the pupil to string, or lace, in a circular manner, as the posts are arranged in a circle. One cord can be strung through the top holes of the posts, and another cord can be laced through the center holes, or the cord can be zigzagged from the top to the center holes to vary the pattern. The final accomplishment is with the "Double Birthday Cake," which has two circles of post, one within the other, on which several patterns may be carried out in increasing complexity.

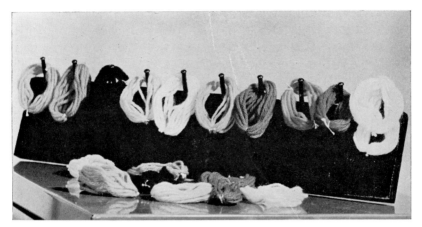

B-8 and B-9. Colored Yarns.

B-8 and B-9. *Colored Yarns (also Shaded)*

OBJECTIVES

1. To develop the ability to distinguish visually among colors.
2. To develop the ability to note similarities and differences.
3. To develop accuracy in manipulative movements.

MATERIALS

Containers holding ten pairs of colored yarns, also boxes with varied pairs of shaded yarns of the same color. Racks with ten nails to hank up the yarns in pairs.

SUBJECT MATTER

Discrimination of color, manual dexterity.

PROCEDURE

Introduce a few of the most contrasting colors first. Hang them on the nails of the rack and ask the pupil to put the matching skeins on top of the one already hanging. Time and efficiency are considered as elements of successful mastery.

After the child is able to successfully match the more contrasting colors, then the shadings of these colors may be introduced.

The child is encouraged to note and correct his own mistakes.

B-10. Inset Puzzles.

B-10. *Inset Puzzles*

OBJECTIVES
1. To develop eye, finger and hand (perceptual-motor) coordination.
2. To aid the child to observe shape, size and color.
3. To aid the child to recognize similarities and differences in shape, size and color.
4. To aid the child to note visual and spatial cues in problem solving.
5. To aid the child to evaluate his own work for errors and corrections.
6. To improve the child's ability to attend to stimuli.

MATERIALS

Ten animal puzzles made of maple wood $\frac{3}{4}''$ thick. The animal forms are approximately $8'' \times 10''$ and $3'' \times 8''$.

SUBJECT MATTER

Visualization of forms.

PROCEDURE

The child is instructed to lay and join the pieces which vary from two to four per puzzle, on the table. The pattern is laid out on the table, or on a guide to the reproduction of the puzzle. Later the child is induced to construct the figures perpendicularly without the pattern. When this is done, the figures are standing animal models.

B-11. *Weight Matching*

OBJECTIVES

1. To develop kinesthetic acuity.
2. To help the child recognize similarities and differences in weight.
3. To strengthen the child's ability to attend.

MATERIALS

A collection of ten small metal boxes containing lead, which are of graduated weight, matched in pairs.

SUBJECT MATTER

Discrimination of weights.

PROCEDURE

When introducing paired weights, we have found it profitable to introduce the extremes first. The child is given one of the heaviest and one of the lightest boxes for comparison until he can rightly connect the meaning of 'heavy' and 'light' with the proper weight.

After he understands that, the child matches the weighted boxes. The teacher presents the problems as follows:

1. The heaviest pair with the next lightest pair.

2. The second heaviest pair with the lightest pair.
3. The middle pair with either the lightest or the heaviest pair.

When progress permits, the third pair should be introduced, making a group of six to be paired. They should consist of the middle pair, the heaviest pair and the next lightest pair. The next combination should be the second heaviest pair, middle and lightest pair.

When problems can be readily solved, the pupil is ready for the fourth pair of the teacher's choice. (**Emphasis:** Each problem should be mastered before the next is presented.)

B-12. *Long and Short*

OBJECTIVES
1. To aid the child to note similarities and differences.
2. To develop spatial orientation.
3. To develop hand manipulation skills.
4. To aid the child to attend to stimuli.

MATERIALS
Table top or board on which are lines painted yellow and green alternately. Wooden slats painted yellow and green in the same lengths as the drawn lines.

SUBJECT MATTER
Discrimination of size; spatial orientation.

PROCEDURE
The teacher asks the child to match the different lengths of colored slats with the lines drawn on the table. The child must fit the colored slats onto the design.

B-13. *Bolt and Nut Board*

OBJECTIVES
1. To develop integration between physical and perceptual functions.
2. To develop fine hand and finger coordination.
3. To develop skill in noting similarities and differences.

4. To develop utilization of the tactile-kinesthetic sensations.
5. To lengthen the child's attention span.

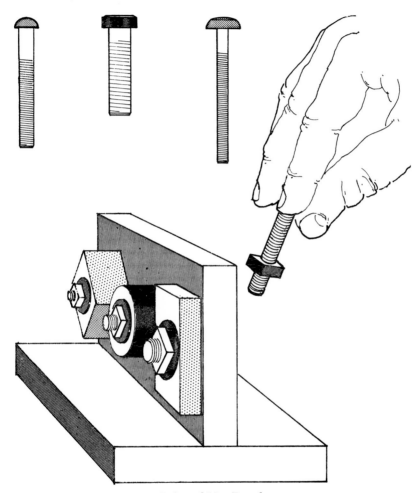

Bolt and Nut Board

MATERIALS

A board 10″ × 12″ × 1″, standing on edge. Holes are bored into the board to receive bolts of different diameters. The selection includes machine, carriage and stove bolts. Matching nuts are provided.

SUBJECT MATTER
Discrimination of size, manual dexterity.

PROCEDURE
Place a bolt through one of the holes in the board. Demonstrate placing the nut on the screw end of the bolt. Then place two other bolts which are in large contrast in size in holes, and have the pupil find the proper nuts to fit those bolts. Proceed to more difficult presentations.

B-14. *Colored Cubes*

OBJECTIVES
1. To develop the ability to perceive color.
2. To develop the ability to note similarities and differences.
3. To improve the child's (hand) manipulative ability.
4. To encourage the child to evaluate his work.

MATERIALS
Colored cubes $1\frac{1}{2}''$ square. Each face is a different color, but all cubes are identical (six faces to cube, six colors). Some faces are colored in two colors, diagonally; some are all one color. Designs to match cube-faces painted on table top. Same designs painted on oil cloth or similar material.

SUBJECT MATTER
Discrimination and identification of color.

PROCEDURE
The teacher turns up one face of a cube; the pupil finds a matching face and turns it up. Later, the child matches the designs painted on the table by placing matching blocks on top of the designs. Finally the difficulty may be increased by hanging the oil cloth design on the wall. The child, still using blocks, reproduces the design on an unmarked table top or other surface.

B-15. *Discs on Nails*

OBJECTIVES
1. To develop physical-perceptual skills.

2. To aid the child to utilize visual and kinesthetic sensations.
3. To lengthen the child's attention span.

MATERIALS
Blocks 4″ × 4″, with one, two or three finishing nails protruding from one face, and $\frac{1}{2}$″ thick discs drilled with one, two or three holes so arranged that they will fit down over the protruding nails.

SUBJECT MATTER
Experience of relationships existing between different objects.

PROCEDURE
The child begins with the one nail block. From the pile of one, two and three-hole discs, he selects those having one hole, and places them on the nail. He proceeds to the two and three-hole discs and the corresponding blocks.

Later, using all three types at once, he places discs, as they come to hand, on appropriate blocks.

B-16. *Skull Pairing*

OBJECTIVES
1. To develop and strengthen the ability to recognize similarities and differences.
2. To aid the child to note small details.
3. To improve hand and finger coordination.
4. To develop the sense of laterality.
5. To develop speed and accuracy in movement and decision making.
6. To lengthen the child's attention span.

MATERIALS
Rack (such as jewelers use to display rings). Small plastic skulls, often used on key chains. These have minor differences, such as one eye or two eyes, eyes of different colors, some with loops, some with part loops, some without loops. There are several boxes, with 8 skulls each, arranged in a series of increasing difficulty such as:
  1. No loop, left eye red
  2. No loop, left eye green

3. No loop, left eye blue
4. No loop, right eye red
5. No loop, right eye green
6. No loop, right eye blue
7. Full loop, right eye red
8. Full loop, right eye green
9. Full loop, right eye blue
10. Full loop, left eye red
11. Full loop, left eye green
12. Full loop, left eye blue
13. $\frac{1}{2}$ loop, right eye green
14. $\frac{1}{2}$ loop, right eye blue
15. $\frac{1}{2}$ loop, right eye red
16. $\frac{1}{2}$ loop, left eye green
17. $\frac{1}{2}$ loop, left eye blue
18. $\frac{1}{2}$ loop, left eye red
19. $\frac{1}{4}$ loop at right, right eye red
20. $\frac{1}{4}$ loop at right, right eye blue
21. $\frac{1}{4}$ loop at right, right eye green
22. $\frac{1}{4}$ loop at left, eye red
23. $\frac{1}{4}$ loop at left, left eye blue
24. $\frac{1}{4}$ loop at left, left eye green

SUBJECT MATTER
Recognition of colors, attention to detail.

PROCEDURE
The skulls in group one, without loops, are presented first. The teacher places four skulls of a series on the rack and requires the child to match these skulls by placing each of the remaining skulls beside its mate on the rack. The skulls are presented in increasing difficulty as the child becomes more proficient.

B-17. *Hidden Objects*
OBJECTIVES
1. To develop integration between perceptual and motor functions.
2. To develop kinesthetic and tactile acuity.
3. To aid the child to note proprioceptive cues.

4. To aid the child to make discriminations.
5. To develop the ability to identify objects by name.
6. To promote language development.

MATERIALS

A bag made of turkish towel. A box 8″ × 14″, 6″ high. Both ends are open; across one hangs a cloth curtain. Twelve boxes 6½″ × 12″, 3″ high. These are closed on all sides but have sliding tops. Each of the smaller boxes contains ten small familiar objects. The objects should be actual, everyday items. Miniatures are not recommended. Contents of twelve boxes used are:

Box one
1. Saucer
2. cup
3. toothbrush
4. comb
5. knife
6. fork
7. spoon
8. scissors (dull)
9. salt shaker
10. bottle

Box two
1. airplane
2. Mask
3. whistle
4. wooden block
5. door knob
6. hammer head
7. sock
8. eyeglasses
9. pencil
10. skate key

Box three
1. golf ball
2. safety pin
3. button
4. soup spoon
5. watch
6. nail
7. chain
8. belt
9. rope
10. skate wheels (2)

Box four
1. razor (blade omitted)
2. paint brush
3. zipper
4. clothes pin
5. medicine dropper
6. bottle top
7. wood screw
8. strap
9. steel washer
10. marble

Box five
1. bean bag
2. bobby pin
3. screw driver
4. wrench
5. clothes hook
6. auger bit
7. file
8. door stop
9. hair brush
10. yo-yo

Box six
1. staple
2. roofing nail
3. door hook
4. iron ring
5. padlock
6. latch
7. pen
8. wire
9. glass
10. light socket

Box seven
1. iron pipe
2. wing nut
3. chair castor
4. razor, safety (closed)
5. bolt and nut
6. buckle
7. hook bolt
8. finishing nail
9. hinge
10. hose coupling

Box eight
1. toy boat
2. hack saw blade
3. fuse plug
4. rock
5. drawer knob
6. screw eye
7. purse
8. three-way electric plug
9. whisk broom
10. round headed screw

Box nine
1. yarn
2. match book
3. sandpaper
4. hose washer
5. flashlight bulb
6. pulley
7. die (one of pair dice)
8. toggle bolt
9. spiral spring
10. top

Box ten
1. clamshell
2. domino
3. insulator
4. cement nail
5. copper rivet
6. key
7. earring
8. hasp
9. sleigh bell
10. sponge rubber

Box eleven
1. jar lid
2. conduit
3. glass cutter
4. turnbuckle
5. battery
6. acorn
7. bone
8. can opener
9. harness snap
10. thimble

Box twelve
1. pine cone
2. egg-beater
3. gear
4. aspirin box
5. doll
6. chalk
7. rattle cube
8. bracelet
9. hose coupling
10. hose clamp

SUBJECT MATTER
Identification and recognition of objects through the tactile sense.

PROCEDURE
The large box is placed on the table between teacher and child, with the curtained side of the box facing the child. The teacher puts the first of the small boxes (which contains the most simple objects) into the large box. The child is asked to put his hands under the curtain, reach into the box, take one object, manipulate it, and tell the teacher its name before he is allowed to see it. This

procedure is continued until all of the objects in the box have been identified. As the objects are correctly identified, they are taken from the box and placed before the child. The process is continued until all twelve boxes have been presented. The children are helped to pronounce the names of the objects if necessary.

Later, after the child has become proficient at the first procedure, the listed objects are placed, one at a time, in a turkish towel bag. The child identifies each object by feeling it through the towel bag.

B-18. *Mosaic Puzzles*

OBJECTIVES

1. To develop the ability to see relationships in terms of size, position, color, and shape of objects.
2. To develop the ability to move from the concrete to the abstract.
3. To help the child to note similarities and differences.
4. To aid the child to evaluate his own work for errors and corrections.
5. To develop speed and accuracy in carrying out activities.

MATERIALS

A variety of geometrical figures made of wood $\frac{1}{2}''$ thick. These vary in size and color as well as in the size of the angles (up to 90°) which form the basis of the geometrical patterns. An oil cloth on which are painted designs to match each of the geometrical figures.

Suggested Sets

1. 6 pieces — 4 pattern sheets — 5 designs
2. 8 pieces — 1 pattern sheet — 2 designs
3. 30 pieces — 3 pattern sheets — 4 designs
4. 16 pieces — 2 pattern sheets — 4 designs
5. 11 pieces — 2 pattern sheets — 2 designs
6. 20 pieces — 2 pattern sheets — 3 designs
7. 25 pieces — 1 pattern sheet — 2 designs
8. 21 pieces — 1 pattern sheet — 1 design
9. 22 pieces — 1 pattern sheet — 2 designs
10. 23 pieces — 1 pattern sheet — 1 design
11. 33 pieces — 2 pattern sheets — 2 designs
12. 42 pieces — 1 pattern sheet — 1 design

13. 50 pieces — 2 pattern sheets — 4 designs
14. 41 pieces — 4 pattern sheets — 5 designs
15. 28 pieces — 2 pattern sheets — 2 designs

SUBJECT MATTER

Exercise and development of visual discrimination through manipulation of form objects.

PROCEDURE

At first the pupils work on the oilcloth puzzle patterns laid out (horizontally) on the table. The pupil covers each picture design with the mosaic piece of identical color, shape and size. After he has gained proficiency, the picture is hung on the wall (vertically). Now the child reproduces the design on the horizontal plane of the table while looking at the vertical pattern. He proceeds through the entire series again in this way.

B-19. *Pyramid Mosaic Puzzles*

OBJECTIVES

1. To develop the ability to see relationships in terms of position, color, size, and shape.
2. To develop the ability to move from the concrete to the abstract.
3. To help the child to note similarities and differences.
4. To stimulate the child to evaluate his own work for errors and corrections.
5. To develop speed and accuracy in carrying out activities.

MATERIALS

Formboards on which are painted horizontal strips all of the same width (1 inch), but of different lengths and colors. A supply of slats of wood, 1″ wide and ½″ thick, of lengths and colors to

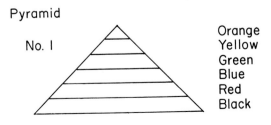

Pyramid

No. I

Orange
Yellow
Green
Blue
Red
Black

Triangles

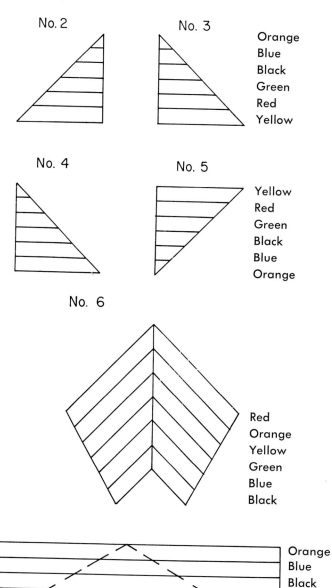

No. 2   No. 3

Orange
Blue
Black
Green
Red
Yellow

No. 4   No. 5

Yellow
Red
Green
Black
Blue
Orange

No. 6

Red
Orange
Yellow
Green
Blue
Black

Orange
Blue
Black
Green
Red
Yellow

match the painted strips. (The backs of these slats are of an identical, neutral color.) Samples of formboards 1 to 7 are shown in the illustrations after B-19.

SUBJECT MATTER
Visual discrimination through manipulation of form objects.

PROCEDURE
Start with Formboard #1. The pupil places the appropriate slats on the strips. He later builds pyramids on Formboards 2 and 3 in the same manner. The child may reverse the pyramids as shown in Nos. 4 and 5.

In No. 7 he builds a rectangle of many colored strips of varying lengths over the entire board (see illustration). For this difficult task the pupil takes the longest slat, #1, and places it horizontally at the bottom of the formboard. Then he takes two shorter pieces, (a and b), of the same color as slat #1, and places one at each end of slat #1. Next, he places slat #2 immediately above slat #1, and places two shorter pieces (c and d), one at each end of slat #2, in order to complete the second level (from the bottom) of the rectangle. This is continued until all the strips are filled. (In each successive strip level, the center section becomes shorter, and the end pieces correspondingly longer.)

After the pupil masters this task he builds patterns No. 1 to 7 from memory without the formboards.

B-20. *All Around Device (Calliope)*

OBJECTIVES
1. To develop visual and auditory discrimination.
2. To aid in the development of ear training.
3. To aid in the development of color identification and discrimination.
4. To strengthen the child's ability to attend to auditory stimuli.

MATERIALS
The "calliope" is a wooden chest, 10″ × 12″ × 22″. The chest, which is designed so that it can be used out of doors, opens at the

side, but is so arranged that after opening, it is stood on one end with the opened face towards the teacher (as illustrated). On the front side of the "calliope" are various apertures and a radio loudspeaker.

B-20. All Around Device (Calliope).

Inside, the chest contains several apparatuses. It is wired for a radio, buzzer, light bulbs, electric bell, chimes, fan and a transformer. Here also are fixed a bicycle horn, a rattle, a child's snapping "cricket" device, holiday noise maker, hand bells, duck call, chimes and electric wall outlet. The chest also holds a rotating glass jar containing a piece of translucent paper on which are printed words, pictures and bits of variously colored paper. A bulb is installed in the jar. Thus, when the jar is rotated the desired color, words or pictures are projected through the apertures on the front of the "calliope."

SUBJECT MATTER

Visual and auditory perception and discrimination.

PROCEDURE

The teacher may first work on color. He assigns a specific color to each child to identify. For example: John gets red, Patty blue, etc. By manipulating the jar, the teacher then flashes the colors. The child does not need to name the color, but only raises his hand when his assigned color appears.

In the same manner, each child is assigned a specific sound to identify when it is produced.

For a third activity, colored ribbon streamers are fixed on the rim of the fan opening. Each pupil is asked to catch a designated fluttering streamer between his finger and thumb when the fan is turned on.

The radio is for background music.

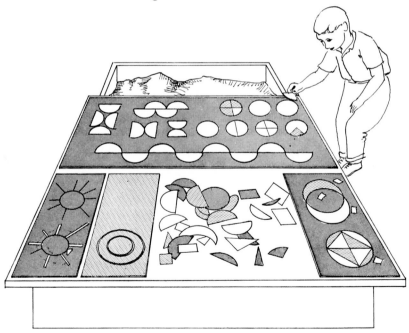

B-21. Arcs and Angles.

B-21. *Arcs and Angles*

OBJECTIVES

1. To develop form perception in the child.
2. To aid the child to note likenesses and differences.
3. To develop manual dexterity.
4. To lengthen the child's attention span.
5. To aid the child to evaluate his own work for errors and corrections.

MATERIALS

Various abstract forms, differing in color, shape and size, painted on sheets of masonite (see illustration) . Forms consist of squares, rectangles, triangles, ovals, circles and ellipses. Cutouts to match the painted forms in color, size and shape.

SUBJECT MATTER

Perception of forms and colors.

PROCEDURE

The teacher places the simplest pattern in front of the child on a table, and asks him to cover each part of the pattern with the matching form, considering shape, size and color. If the pupil succeeds, continue with the more difficult patterns. This exercise compliments, with arcs, the angles of *Mosaic Puzzles* (**B-18**).

B-22. *Coat of Arms*

OBJECTIVES

1. To develop hand manipulation and general physical coordination skills.
2. To develop the ability to visualize and discriminate between objects.
3. To improve the child's skill in bodily movement.
4. To give the child the experience of possession.
5. To develop recognition of the property rights of others.

MATERIALS

The "Coats of Arms" are made out of circular pieces of $\frac{3}{4}''$ plywood, 14″ in diameter. In the center of each disc is a hole $1\frac{1}{2}''$

in diameter. On each "Coat of Arms" there is a painted design and the name of the pupil to whom it belongs.

SUBJECT MATTER
Body movement; recognition of objects.

PROCEDURE
Every child in the group is the owner of one of the "Coats of Arms." The discs are used in various ways: the children can sit on the discs if the ground is wet or cold; as an exercise in accuracy, the pupils practice rolling the discs along a straight track; or in a contest, the teacher rolls the discs one at a time, and each child is asked to catch his own "Coat of Arms;" the discs are stacked, and a pupil is asked to distribute them, without help or cues, to their respective owners.

B-23. *Knot Tying and Knot Untying*

OBJECTIVES
1. To develop manual dexterity.
2. To develop physical-perceptual coordination.
3. To aid the child to note similarities and differences.
4. To develop the ability to attend to stimuli.

MATERIALS
Smooth curtain cord in one yard lengths. Heavy wrapping string. Colored cotton warp. Knitting yarn. Colored thread.

SUBJECT MATTER
Physical-perceptual coordination, manipulation.

PROCEDURE
Allow the child to untie simple knots at first, and gradually develop the ability to handle difficult knots. Smooth curtain cord is first used with loose knots. As progress indicates, knots are tightened and made more difficult (for example, by tangling knitting yarn and silk thread together) . Two to five strands are used; colors are used to trace position of strings.

B-24. *Dressing Techniques* **and**
B-25. *Shoe Lacing*

OBJECTIVES
1. To develop manual dexterity.
2. To aid the child in assuming responsibility for his self care.
3. To aid the child to identify the various dressing techniques: lacing, tying, buttoning, etc.
4. To lengthen the child's attention span.

MATERIALS
Forms made of cloth-covered porous rubber on which are sewn various kinds of buttons, zippers, snaps, hooks and eyes. Weighted cement footforms and shoes, shoe laces.

SUBJECT MATTER
Dressing skills.

PROCEDURE
The child holds forms, one at a time, against his body, to simulate clothing, and proceeds to practice buttoning, zipping, etc. In shoe lacing, he practices with the toe of the shoe pointed away from his body. Also, when kneeling on chair with one leg, the pupil practices with the shoe in front of his knee, again with the toe of the shoe pointing away from his body.

B-26. *Noise Cage*

OBJECTIVES
1. To aid the child to establish connection between something he does and something that happens as a result of what he does.
2. To develop the child's own initiative in discovering the unusual for himself and of himself.
3. To develop manual dexterity.
4. To stimulate the child to seek additional experience in his environment.
5. To strengthen the child's ability to attend to auditory stimuli.

B-26. Noise Cage.

MATERIALS

A cylinder of $\frac{1}{4}''$ mesh rabbit wire. 24" long, and 15" diameter, having wooden ends. It is 15" off the ground, supported by an axle. This permits it to turn horizontally. It contains the proper amount of small pieces of plastic to produce a loud, shocking clatter when turned.

SUBJECT MATTER
Awareness of sounds. To cause *something* to happen.

PROCEDURE
The child is permitted to explore the area in which this device is
located. It is hoped that the child will *discover* the capacity of the
cylinder to turn when pushed, and that he will note the sounds so
produced.

B-27. *Bell Ringing*

OBJECTIVES
1. To develop auditory discrimination skills.
2. To aid the child to establish connection between something
   he does and something that happens as a result of what he does.
3. To develop and arouse natural curiosity.
4. To develop the ability to initiate activities.

B-27. Bell Ringing.

MATERIALS
Series of fifteen bicycle bells which differ slightly in pitch. These are fastened to fence or wall.

SUBJECT MATTER
Discrimination of sounds.

PROCEDURE
This device makes use of whatever natural curiosity the child might have. The child is permitted to "explore" the area immediate to the bells and may be attracted by their brightness, their appearance, their location, or whatever. He is permitted, encouraged, and, if necessary, shown the bells and their capacities demonstrated. Further opportunities for this experience are provided. The differences in pitch can then be pointed out and the pleasant result of the child's action reinforced by praise.

B-28. Masks and Bells.

B-28. *Masks and Bells*

OBJECTIVES
1. To develop an auditory awareness.
2. To develop the ability to discriminate sound on a spatial dimension.
3. To aid the child to initiate self-direction. (By attending to the origin of the sound.)

MATERIALS
Facial masks which cover the eyes. One bell.

SUBJECT MATTER
Sensory awareness of sound, awareness of position in relation to the source of the sound (positionality).

PROCEDURE
A member of a group of children is provided with a mask. Another child is given the bell, and remains in one place. Desks and chairs are disordered to act as a maze. The masked child is turned around a few times, and urged to note the direction from which the bell is sounded and to go to the source. The extra pupils are grouped out of the way near a wall. Each pupil is masked in turn.

B-29. *Sound Matching*

OBJECTIVES
1. To develop auditory acuity.
2. To provide experiences in noting differences in pitch, tone, and volume.
3. To provide kinesthetic experiences through manipulation of objects.
4. To aid the child to establish connection between something he does and something that happens as a result of what he does.

MATERIALS
A collection of small boxes, pairs of which are filled with the following materials: rice, flour, split peas, beans, paper clips, etc. The amounts in the containers are also matched in pairs.

SUBJECT MATTER
Discrimination of sounds.

PROCEDURE
The sound boxes are introduced as three boxes, one pair loud and distinctive, and a single box with a soft, muffled sound. The teacher shakes one of the loud boxes for the pupil to listen to. Then the child determines, by shaking the other two boxes in turn, which of the two matches the one the teacher shook, to make the pair. He gives his choice to the teacher. As another task, the student is given one box of a pair to shake as he compares it to the other boxes before him.

B-29. Sound Matching.

As soon as he understands what is expected of him, a box which produces a sound markedly different from the others is added to the first three boxes. When the student becomes proficient at distinguishing the sounds made by these boxes, a fifth box with yet another sound is added. As he progresses, more sound boxes are added.

B-30. *Carillon Pipes*

OBJECTIVES
1. To develop the child's auditory perceptual ability.
2. To encourage the child to note similarities and differences in sounds.
3. To aid the child to appreciate melodic sounds.
4. To aid the child to establish connection between something he does and something that happens as a result of what he does.
5. To encourage the child to exercise his curiosity.

MATERIALS
The apparatus consists of nine different chrome metal pipes, which can be hung on a fence or wall. Of varying lengths, the pipes produce tones which are different enough, one from the other, to be easily recognized.

SUBJECT MATTER
Auditory recognition and discrimination.

PROCEDURE
The child is allowed to discover and/or strike the pipes by "accident." Curiosity should lead him to strike each pipe, to enjoy the sounds it produces, and to discover the variety of sounds possible. This should aid him also to note the "cause and effect" element of his acts.

B-31. *Tone Counting*

OBJECTIVES
1. To develop the child's auditory perceptual ability.
2. To improve the child's auditory memory.
3. To provide experiences in counting.
4. To strengthen the child's ability to attend to auditory stimuli.

MATERIALS
A large metal bell and a large nail or metal bar. Data sheets on which to keep the child's record.

SUBJECT MATTER
Auditory discrimination and counting.

PROCEDURE
The teacher sits behind the child and strikes the bell slowly, from one to ten times, as desired. Rhythmic patterns may be varied, depending upon the ability of the individual. Ask the child how many times the bell was hit each time. Record the answers.

B-32. *Treasure Hunt*

OBJECTIVES
1. To develop the child's visual perceptual ability.
2. To aid the child to note likenesses and differences of objects.
3. To aid the child to develop spatial discrimination.

MATERIALS
Small objects arranged, in pairs, in boxes. The objects include items such as bracelets, trinkets, key charms, and words printed on pieces of wood or masonite.

SUBJECT MATTER
Development of spatial-perceptual orientation through recognition of likenesses and differences.

PROCEDURE
Objects are placed about the room. The child is given their mates, one at a time, and is asked to find the matching objects. At the beginning, objects are placed in sight, later in concealed places. Begin with the simpler objects and proceed to the more complex ones.

B-33. *Over and Under*

OBJECTIVES
1. To develop the child's quantitative concepts.
2. To develop the child's ability to count.
3. To provide the child with an opportunity to take turns and to cooperate with others.

MATERIALS

A game board made of masonite, rectangular in shape. On it are painted two rectangles, one bearing the legend "under 7," the other "over 7." Between these two rectangles, in the center of the game board, is painted "7." Example:

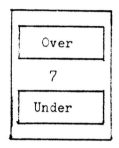

Two cubes with Arabic numerals on their sides (in the manner of dice), a supply of small plastic discs or chips.

SUBJECT MATTER

Noting quantitative relationships.

PROCEDURE

Two or more children can play the game. The children make their selection for "under 7," "over 7" or plain "7." Each child is provided with a number of chips all of one color. He places his chips within the lines of the box of his choice. The teacher throws the cube. If it turns up a number "under 7" the children who chose that box divide the chips placed in the other boxes. (The teacher makes up any inadequacy in the number of chips from the bank.) The same procedure applies if the total is "over 7." But if the dice count is "7," ten more chips from the "bank" are added to the sum of the chips in the other boxes for division among those who chose "7." The ones with the most chips at end of play period are the winners.

B-34. Barber Pole

OBJECTIVES

1. To develop physical-perceptual coordination.

2. To provide large muscle exercises.
3. To aid the child to improve postural adjustment.
4. To develop the child's spatial perception ability to accurately judge short distances.

MATERIALS

A $2\frac{1}{2}''$ steel pipe, painted red and white, $5'5''$ high standing upright in a concrete base $15''$ in diameter. Ten inches of the base are below ground surface which leaves $2''$ above ground to act as a foot brace. Cotton web belt $1\frac{3}{4}''$ wide and from $6'$ to to $8'$ long. It is riveted at one end to a large bronze friction buckle.

SUBJECT MATTER

Cross motor coordination.

PROCEDURE

Begin with caution. Stand pupil upon concrete base $6''$ to $8''$ from pole with a loop that encloses pupil and pole. Pupil leans back with whole body while heels are together with pole between his feet. All the while the pupil holds the belt, with both hands, waist high. While still leaning away from pole he travels in a circle around the pole by pushing with feet and by leaning and swaying in desired direction. As skill and courage develop, the loop is gradually lengthened. It will become necessary for the insteps or arches to be placed against the rim of the base, heels touching the ground.

Most children can operate at a 45 degree angle. Teach pupils to go fast and slow and how to revolve from left to right. When pupil can work in wide circles, five or more may use the pole at the same time. In the interests of safety, point out to them the importance of holding the belt tightly at the double thickness where surplus web comes through the buckle.

B-35. *Versatile Sticks*

OBJECTIVES

1. To develop the spatial sense in the child.
2. To demonstrate the application of noting similarities and differences as a means of problem solving.

3. To develop ability to match objects by color, size, shape, and number of objects.
4. To develop ability to sort objects.
5. To develop imagination and creativity.
6. To demonstrate the element of fun in learning.

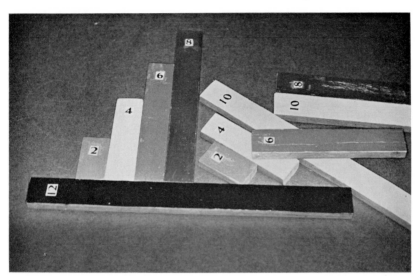

B-35. Versatile Sticks.

MATERIALS
A set of eleven sticks consisting of five pairs of different lengths, colors and numbers and one odd stick 12″ long and of black color. The pairs are painted orange, red, blue, green, and yellow, and are 2″, 4″, 6″, 8″, and 10″ long with a numeral indicating its length on the end of each stick. The backside of the sticks are unpainted or of one color different from the frontside colors.

SUBJECT MATTER
Perception of size, shape, color, position. Number relations.

PROCEDURE
The teacher and pupil sit on the same side of the table.
1. Matching: arrange all sticks in pairs; first by color, then by length, with colored face down and last, by numbers, placing the numbered ends together.

2. To demonstrate length, the 12″ stick is placed horizontally before the child, colored side down. The 8″ stick is placed on the near side of the 12″ stick so that their sides are touching and with their left ends even. At the right end of the 8″ stick, place a 4″ stick in the same position.

There are not two 12″ sticks. Explain that both sticks are long. Remove the 4″ stick and explain that one stick is long, and the other is short. Replace the short stick and explain that both are long. Do the same with the other sticks in relation to the 12″ stick.

Repeat the same procedure by showing this same relation between the other sticks (for instance, compare the 6″ stick with other sticks). Show that two, three and four sticks can equal the length of a longer one.

As variations, use sticks in same order while they are placed in vertical position or with right ends even.

3. To teach the difference between "high and low," demonstrate by holding sticks on end in upright position.

4. To demonstrate beadth (wide and narrow): Place the 12″ stick in vertical position in front of the players, on a strip of paper 6″ long and 2 to 4″ wide, the length of which is at a right angle to the stick. Explain that the stick is narrow. Place a pair of sticks, totaling 12″ in length, beside the 12″ stick. Show that the stick width grows wider and wider as additional pairs are placed together until the paper is covered. As sticks are removed, in pairs, explain that the sticks grow narrow.

Repeat all while using sticks in vertical plane.

5. Exercise in pattern building and positional relationships. All sticks are placed with colored face up. Each stick must be placed at either right angles or parallel to another stick in the pattern being built. Each stick must touch another stick; no stick can be isolated.

Only the teacher may move the 12″ stick up or down.

A stick may be picked up when changing position.

6. Sorting: Use the 6″ stick as measurement and let the longer sticks be put to one side and the shorter ones to the other; or place the sorted sticks in containers.

7. The game action: the 12″ stick is placed in front of teacher and pupil in vertical position midway between these two players.

   Each player has one of each of the pairs, colored face up. The teacher starts the play by placing a stick against the central 12″ stick, either parallel or perpendicular to it.

   The pupil follows play by placing matching color in the corresponding place on his side of the dividing 12″ stick. When all sticks are placed, the play is continued by moving the sticks to other places.

   By taking turns a constantly changing and symmetrical picture can be built.

   When game is thoroughly understood, it can be played by placing the 12″ stick in horizontal plane.

   An interesting and more difficult variation can be played. The 12″ stick is placed vertically between the players. The pupil uses one end of the 12″ stick and the teacher the other. In this play, the teacher's sticks will point down and the pupil's sticks will point up.

   This version can also be played by placing the 12″ stick in horizontal plane.

8. Number knowledge. Start by placing the stick number ten beside and touching horizontally stick number twelve which is in a horizontal position between the players. Numbered ends should be on the right.

   On the end of the number ten stick place the number two stick and show that the two sticks are equal to twelve. Repeat this procedure by using sticks with numbers six and six. Use other combinations of two sticks to total twelve.

   Variation (for use only when names of numerals are known) : place end to end any two sticks with a number total of twelve or less. Then find, by measuring, a single stick of same length. Show that the numbers of the pair total the same as the one long stick.

   Subtraction: for this procedure, use a single stick with a length equal to two others. Show that, for instance, by taking four away from twelve, eight will remain and that by taking away eight, four will remain.

   Use other combinations of three sticks.

ADVANCED PHYSICAL-PERCEPTUAL SKILLS

Units of Instruction

THE GOAL OF THE third stage of the functional teaching program is to help the pupils draw conclusions and make decisions based on early as well as new experiences. In this phase, the pupils meet sensory stimuli in a context which requires them to structure and to generalize their impressions. The following exercises require the ranking and matching of stimuli in more elaborate ways and for more complicated assignments than were needed in the previous two stages of the Program. Identification of numbers, letters and words are additional skills developed by the exercises included in this section. The material in this section is related to the discussion in Chapter 6.

C-1. *Framed Inset Puzzles*

OBJECTIVES
1. To develop physical-perceptual coordination.
2. To aid the child to observe shape, size and color.
3. To aid the child to recognize similarities and differences in shape, size and color among objects.
4. To aid the child to evaluate his own work for errors and corrections.
5. To develop the child's ability to work with increasing accuracy.
6. To improve the child's ability to attend to stimuli.

MATERIALS
Ordinary jig-saw type puzzles, each containing four pieces, set in wooden frames. The pieces of the puzzle, when correctly put together, complete a picture. The edges of the pieces, and their corresponding frame edges are painted in matching colors. The backs of the puzzle pieces and the backs of the frame are also colored so that when the whole frame is turned over, each piece and the part of the frame which borders it are of identical color.

132

SUBJECT MATTER
Manipulation of objects according to size, shape, form and color.

PROCEDURE
The puzzle board is placed before the child with the pieces mixed. He is encouraged to fit the blocks with the picture side up first. This may be done by piecing the picture together or by matching colored edges to colored edges of the frame and related parts. After several series are completed, turn the puzzle boards over. Ask the child to see if the colored pieces match the colored frame of the reverse side. If the pieces fit on one side, they most certainly will match on the other side.

C-2. *Race Horses*

OBJECTIVES
1. To develop the ability to count, using abstract symbols.
2. To develop speed and accuracy in counting.
3. To develop the spatial sense in the child.
4. To provide social experiences, such as cooperation and interdependence in taking turns and helping each other.

MATERIALS
A special die with both dots and arabic numerals from 1 to 6, or a spin dial. A masonite board, cloth, or table, the top marked as in drawing shown below. (We have two painted on our table.)

6

5

4

3

2

1

SUBJECT MATTER
Counting.

PROCEDURE
Two to twelve children line up to play race horses. Each child is assigned a number, beginning with 1 and provided with a figure of a horse or a colored block. The rolling of the die or spinning the dial may be done in a number of ways, at the teacher's discretion. The children may do it, in rotation; the teacher may do it at all times; or the child whose horse has just advanced may do it. For the sake of illustration, perhaps the teacher throws the die for the first play, and 3 turns up. The player to whom 3 has been assigned advances his horse one space. Then he rolls the die, and 1 comes up. Player 1 advances his horse 1 space and then rolls the die. The pupil who gets to the end of the board first wins the "race." The teacher should encourage the child to note the Arabic numerals first, and later to note the dots of die.

Version No. 2. In this version, each child throws the die in turn. The number each player turns up (e.g., "3") is the number of spaces his horse may be advanced. But at the end, the player must throw the number which matches exactly the remaining spaces. He must remain in his space, taking his regular turn, until he throws the required number. When the two race courses are used, dice used are numbered 1 through 12.

C-3. *Jumping Peg ("Peggy")*

OBJECTIVES
1. To develop manual dexterity.
2. To develop the ability to identify colors.
3. To develop the ability to count.
4. To develop spatial perception.
5. To encourage interaction in a group situation.

MATERIALS
Ten or more slats $8'' \times 1'' \times 1''$ in assorted colors and ten slats $8'' \times \frac{3}{4}'' \times \frac{1}{2}''$, also in different colors. All slats are numbered on one side.

One wooden piece $1''$ high $\times \frac{3}{4}''$ thick, $3''$ in length at top, $2''$ long on base, which is referred to as "Peggy."

SUBJECT MATTER

Manipulation of colored objects to increasing levels of difficulty.

C-3. Jumping Peg ("Peggy").

PROCEDURE

The teacher sets one of the slats at the wider side in position and puts "Peggy" on one side of the slat. She taps "Peggy" with her forefinger so that it will jump over the slat. She asks the child to do this. When the child succeeds, she puts another of the slats at the wider side on top of the first one, and encourages the pupil to make "Peggy" jump over the higher obstacles. She proceeds in this way, first with the wide side of the slats, later with the narrow side to increase difficulty in the build-up of the obstacles by the pupil. Let the pupil select by color through one run, and by numbers through another run, if he has mastered numbers.

C-4. *Pattern Column*

OBJECTIVES

1. To develop physical-perceptual coordination.

2. To develop the child's ability to note visual and tactile sensations.
3. To develop the ability to perceive similarities and differences.
4. To introduce the concept of order and symmetry.
5. To improve the child's ability to attend to stimuli.
6. To emphasize profitable use of leisure time.

MATERIALS

A number of square wooden bases $6\frac{1}{2}'' \times 6\frac{1}{2}'' \times 1''$, with centered spindles $12''$ high. Discs $3''$ in diameter and $\frac{5}{8}''$ thick which can be stacked and revolved upon the spindle. A nut on the top of the spindle makes it possible to remove the discs or to lock them in.

The $\frac{5}{8}''$ edges of the discs are painted with perpendicular stripes of many colors and widths. When brought into proper position on the spindle the short stripes of the many discs mesh to make continuous unbroken lines. In addition, there is a series of cardboard and plastic bands which fit over the discs. When these discs are placed upon the spindle in proper sequence, they can be revolved and aligned upon the spindle to complete pictures, words, letters, numerals, or designs.

SUBJECT MATTER

Physical-perceptual skills: such as discrimination, matching of colors and shapes, and finger dexterity.

PROCEDURE

The teacher demonstrates, with two or three discs, how the discs are arranged to bring the colors or parts to their proper position. The teacher then revolves the discs to disarrange the pattern and gives the apparatus to the child for proper arrangement. Add discs to problem as success indicates. When child thoroughly understands what is expected of him show him the advantage of using both hands, one hand for holding work in place and the other for arranging pattern.

C-5. *Miniature Maze*

OBJECTIVES

1. To develop manual dexterity and coordination.

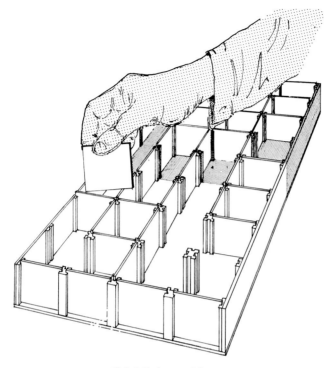

C-5. Miniature Maze.

2. To develop the utilization of visual and tactile senses.
3. To develop spatial perception.
4. To provide an opportunity for social interaction and competition.

MATERIALS

A miniature model of the large walking maze (see D-17). It is rectangular in shape with thirty-two to forty sections which are made of posts and movable panels. Each panel is $2'' \times 3''$. The whole maze is divided into three sections, each a specific color, so that one, two or three sections can be used at a time. A number of chips.

PROCEDURE

Two or more children can participate. Each pupil receives an equal number of panels and a quantity of chips of distinctive color and/or shape. The base is presented: one child is required to place one panel in the grooves of the posts; another child follows up by placing one of his panels between two other posts.

C-6. *Electric Maze*

OBJECTIVES
1. To develop physical-perceptual coordination.
2. To develop fine manual dexterity and coordination.
3. To aid the child to utilize kinesthetic and visual sensations.
4. To improve the child's ability to note spatial relationships.
5. To improve the ability to attend to stimuli.

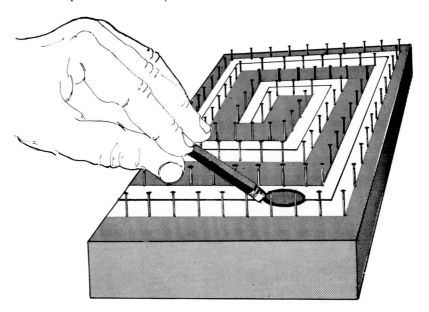

MATERIALS
A maze built into a wooden box 14″ × 10″ × 3″. There is a metal track, or path, which is connected to an electric circuit and outlined with nails which are wired to a buzzer and a transformer. Small and large washers, a nickel, a dime and a quarter.

SUBJECT MATTER
Eye-hand coordination. Manual dexterity.

PROCEDURE

The child is first instructed to push a small washer down the center of the path with a pencil without touching the nails which outline the path. The teacher may demonstrate first. After the pupil gains proficiency, the size of the washer is increased. Later, a disc without a center hole, or a coin may be used. If the child allows the disc to touch a nail he causes a buzzer to ring, and must start again.

C-7. *Arithmetic Problem Boards*

OBJECTIVES

1. To introduce number concepts to the child.
2. To aid the child to deal systematically with abstract symbols.
3. To aid the child to note associations between various abstract perceptions.
4. To aid the child to evaluate his own work for errors and corrections.

MATERIALS

Masonite boards $8'' \times 10'' \times \frac{1}{8}''$ on which are painted three or four columns of arithmetic examples with blank spaces opposite each example for an answer. The boards are painted with chalk-

C-7. Arithmetic Problem Boards (with number columns).

board paint; the problems overlaid in regular paint. Chalk. A damp sponge to clean the board. A list of words and/or symbols that are used in addition, subtraction, and multiplication such as:

Addition	*Subtraction*	*Multiplication*
Add	Subtract	Multiply
$+$	$-$	$\times$
Plus	Minus	Times
Equals	Equals	Equals
More	Less	
Add to	Take Away	

SUBJECT MATTER
Solution of increasingly difficult arithmetical examples.

PROCEDURE
The teacher should first check on the pupil's ability to add simple facts. (If he needs additional help, the work with the Number Sequence Board (C-38) should be continued.) Then, she introduces the simple one-place addition, for instance, $1 + 4 = ?$ The child writes the correct answer in the appropriate empty box and proceeds to the next problem.

After the simple addition columns have been mastered (use for this purpose the **Number Columns (C-40)**) the combinations which require the process of carrying one into ten's place are introduced. Later give combinations where totals carry over to tens and hundreds place.

After efficiency has been developed in adding one and two-place numbers which require carrying one, simple three-place numbers which do not require carrying are introduced. The zero factor may be introduced at this level also.

For subtraction, similar boards are used. Simple facts are worked with first, and gradually, problems which require "borrowing" are introduced.

In multiplication only a few of the simple combinations are taught, providing the child has the ability or shows the readiness to comprehend the process of multiplication.

In addition and subtraction the examples are presented first in horizontal arrangement. They are later presented in vertical arrangement.

EXAMPLES:

4 + 1 =		3 + 5 =	
2 + 2 =		3 + 2 =	
3 + 2 =		2 + 3 =	
2 + 1 =		3 + 3 =	
3 + 2 =		3 + 2 =	
4 + 1 =		4 + 2 =	
1 + 4 =		2 + 4 =	
2 + 2 =		5 + 1 =	
1 + 3 =		3 + 2 =	
2 + 3 =		2 + 3 =	

6 + 1 =		3 + 5 =	
5 + 2 =		5 + 4 =	
1 + 6 =		6 + 5 =	
5 + 1 =		7 + 3 =	
4 + 3 =		8 + 2 =	
3 + 4 =		9 + 2 =	
1 + 6 =		2 + 9 =	
3 + 3 =		7 + 4 =	
5 + 2 =		8 + 3 =	
4 + 3 =		9 + 2 =	

Units added to units and tens

26 + 4 =		36 + 4 =	
15 + 5 =		18 + 2 =	
13 + 7 =		27 + 3 =	
34 + 6 =		26 + 4 =	
53 + 7 =		23 + 7 =	
37 + 3 =		22 + 8 =	
18 + 2 =		21 + 9 =	
26 + 5 =		36 + 4 =	
38 + 2 =		47 + 3 =	
35 + 5 =		58 + 2 =	

Carry over one or more to tens

27 + 4 =		48 + 4 =	
13 + 8 =		85 + 7 =	
62 + 9 =		96 + 6 =	
30 + 40 =		76 + 6 =	
38 + 4 =		35 + 8 =	
38 + 7 =		44 + 8 =	
86 + 15 =		53 + 7 =	
38 + 4 =		63 + 8 =	
29 + 4 =		56 + 6 =	
35 + 6 =		87 + 4 =	

Carry over one from units

66 + 4 =		61 + 9 =	
64 + 6 =		74 + 6 =	
74 + 6 =		36 + 4 =	
83 + 7 =		29 + 1 =	
92 + 8 =		42 + 8 =	
88 + 2 =		57 + 3 =	
93 +7 =		46 + 4 =	
84 + 6 =		18 + 2 =	
77 + 4 =		17 + 3 =	
76 + 4 =		27 + 3 =	

Carry over one   Adding two units and two ten's, no carry over

26 + 4 =		44 + 44 =	
15 + 5 =		65 + 34 =	
13 + 7 =		35 + 14 =	
34 + 6 =		43 + 16 =	
53 + 7 =		71 + 22 =	
47 + 3 =		13 + 86 =	
18 + 2 =		34 + 65 =	
26 + 4 =		14 + 35 =	
38 + 2 =		16 + 43 =	
35 + 5 =		22 + 71 =	

Tens and units-carry over from units

72 + 39 =		12 + 99 =	
53 + 57 =		53 + 57 =	
68 + 52 =		89 + 22 =	
86 + 24 =		86 + 24 =	
43 + 76 =		73 + 38 =	
76 + 34 =		76 + 35 =	
35 + 75 =		66 + 54 =	
87 + 23 =		53 + 47 =	
66 + 44 =		66 + 44 =	
56 + 54 =		34 + 77 =	

Introducing zero 3 places

203 + 470 =		37 + 522 =	
200 + 306 =		63 + 420 =	
720 + 203 =		800 + 107 =	
860 + 110 =		70 + 408 =	
703 + 205 =		602 + 200 =	
210 + 360 =		300 + 686 =	
670 + 306 =		440 + 308 =	
430 + 516 =		64 + 725 =	
530 + 250 =		340 + 604 =	
604 + 300 =		524 + 305 =	

C-8 and 9. *Pattern Matching with Various Shapes and Colors*

OBJECTIVES

1. To develop skill in visual discrimination.
2. To develop physical-perceptual coordination in the child.
3. To aid the child to note similarities and differences.
4. To aid the child to evaluate his own work for errors and corrections.
5. To aid the child to develop the ability to think in a logical manner.
6. To develop the ability to attend to stimuli.

MATERIALS

Rectangular pieces of wall paper with geometrical patterns or variously arrayed numbers or letters, pasted on $\frac{1}{4}''$ masonite 3" $\times$ 5". The designs vary in difficulty from the simple to the complex. In the first series there are 26 boxes, each containing ten pairs of cards which are identical in color as well as in design. In the second series there are thirty-three boxes of ten pairs each; the patterns are identical in design but the colors are different.

SUBJECT MATTER

Visual perception.

C-8. Pattern Matching with Various Shapes and Colors.

Many designs ranging from the simple to the complex
patterns.

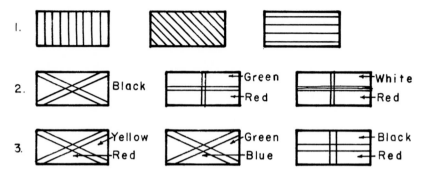

Many designs ranging from the geometrical and floral
patterns.

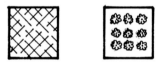

C-9. Pattern Matching.

PROCEDURE

Starting with a box of the simpler cards, the teacher removes two
or more pairs. She gives one card to the pupil and asks him to find
the matching card. Always, each pupil is assigned a specific box
of cards. As his ability and efficiency in matching improves, the
child is required to pair the more difficult designs.

Do not interrupt the child while he is in the process of matching the patterns. After he has finished, check the performance.
If he has made a mistake, let him re-evaluate his own work. This
develops the child's ability not only to note similarities and differences and to concentrate, but also, finally, to reach a conclusion.

C-10. *Pattern Matching with Optical Illusions*

OBJECTIVES

1. To develop visual discrimination skill in the child.

2. To improve skill in noting similarities and differences through identification of various forms.
3. To develop physical-perceptual matching ability.
4. To improve skill in noting attention to detail.

MATERIALS

Ten pairs of cards, 3″ × 5″, each pair illustrating an optical illusion.

Examples

C-10. Pattern Matching with Optical Illusion.

SUBJECT MATTER

Visual perception of drawn forms.

PROCEDURE

The child is asked to match each card with its mate. Do not press the child for a quick performance, but let him discover the features for identification by himself.

C-11. *Pattern Matching (Food Cards)*

OBJECTIVES

1. To develop physical-perceptual skills.
2. To develop discrimination skills in the child.
3. To aid the child to recognize and identify representations of familiar objects.
4. To aid the child to note similarities and differences in visual objects.
5. To improve the ability to attend to visual stimuli.

MATERIALS

Pairs of pictures of various kinds of food, such as vegetables, meats, bread, cake, cookies, and pie, mounted on 2″ × 3″ pieces of masonite.

SUBJECT MATTER
Recognition of similarities and differences.

PROCEDURE
A few common and easily identifiable types of food pictures are presented first. The child is asked to match each card with its mate. When the first cards have been identified, add new cards to the study list.

C-12. Pattern Matching with Photo Cards.

C-12. *Pattern Matching (Photo Cards)*

OBJECTIVES
1. To develop visual discrimination skills in the child.
2. To aid the child to note similarities and differences in detailed material.

3. To develop speed and accuracy in recognition and identification of objects.
4. To aid the child to note detail in visual objects.

MATERIALS
Photographs of persons: some show faces only, some head and bust; others full length, male and female. All are in matched pairs. Photographs are mounted on masonite, and covered with clear lacquer. Size of cards $2'' \times 1\frac{1}{2}''$.

Set No. 1	10 cards		Set No.	6	24 cards
2	20	”		7	24 ”
3	18	”		8	24 ”
4	20	”		9	28 ”
5	20	”		10	28 ”

SUBJECT MATTER
Recognition of similarities and differences.

PROCEDURE
The photographs with faces only are given to the child first. He is asked to discriminate facial features. This continues until the pupil can match these cards with speed and accuracy. Subsequently, the pictures with head and bust are introduced. Later, more detailed full-length photos showing one or two persons can be matched. Speed and accuracy in identification and recognition should be emphasized.

C-13. *Pattern Matching (Automobile Cards)*

OBJECTIVES
1. To develop physical-perceptual skills.
2. To develop visual perceptual skills.
3. To aid the child to note similarities and differences in stimuli.
4. To develop speed and accuracy in recognition and identification of objects.
5. To strengthen the ability to attend.

MATERIALS
A kit containing paired pictures of automobiles. Each kit of cards consists of four groups, each group containing a specific number

of pairs. The cards in each group are identified by colored dots on the backs, for instance, one group is marked with green dots, another with red, the third group is marked with yellow, and the fourth group has blue dots. One card of each pair has one dot, the matching card has two dots. These colored dots enable the teacher to quickly identify the group and so sort the cards in any way she may wish to present them to the children.

SUBJECT MATTER
Recognition of similarities and differences in familiar objects.

PROCEDURE
To begin, the teacher separates pairs by dots. She places two or three cards on the table in front of the child, but holds the matching cards. Then she places one of the matching cards on the table and asks the child to decide which of those cards before him matches the new card.

As the child becomes more proficient in telling 'likes' and 'differences,' he may be given a "group" which is mixed up on the table before him, to sort into matching pairs.

Four children may each be given a group of cards to sort; or one child may be given additional groups to increase the difficulty (by increasing the number of choices possible) until all four groups are in use.

ADDITIONAL PROCEDURE: (Group Game) "Treasure Hunt"
The teacher separates all cards by dot, and places one of each pair in odd places about the classroom. She then deals the matching cards to the children, and tells them to find the mate which is hidden in the room. If the pupil cannot find the mate, he may trade his card for another. The student who finds the most pairs wins the game.

C-14. *Triple Card Matching*

OBJECTIVES
1. To develop physical-perceptual skills.
2. To aid in the development of acute visual perception in the child.

3. To aid the child to note similarities and differences in stimuli.
4. To lengthen the attention span of the child.

MATERIALS

Geometric patterns in triplicate painted on masonite cards $5\frac{1}{2} \times 5\frac{1}{2}''$. The patterns are divided into five groups which vary in shape (circle, squares, ovals, rectangles and polygons) and also vary in the size of the designs and in the circumference (see examples).

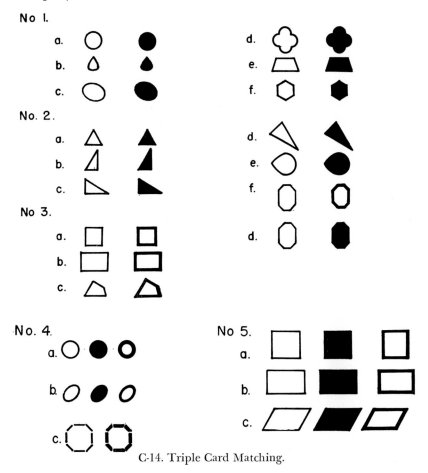

C-14. Triple Card Matching.

SUBJECT MATTER

Perception of identical elements in abstract forms.

PROCEDURE

Start with the simplest designs and ask the child to match patterns. Do not press the child for quick identification, but give him time to find the decisive features for identification. Later proceed to the more difficult designs and triplicates.

C-15. *Going to Town*

OBJECTIVES

1. To stimulate an interest in numbers.
2. To aid in the development of number concepts.
3. To aid in the development of space perception.
4. To aid the child to interpret the meaning of words, phrases and sentences.
5. To emphasize interaction in a group situation and stimulate social relationships for the child.

MATERIALS

A diagram drawn on a table top or masonite board (as shown) and a spinner dial or dice.

SUBJECT MATTER

Recognition of numbers, words. Laterality, directionality.

	1	2	3	4	5	6	7	8	9	10	11	12	13	14	15	16	17
6			Extra Shot				Sneeze		Take 2				Whistle				Take 2
5				Go Back 2							Sneeze			Stand and Turn			
4					Whistle			Subtract 3				Shoot Again		Take 1			
3			Shoot Again							Go Back 3			Stand Up				Whistle
2				Take 3			Miss 1							Call Papa			
1						Cry					Pet the Cat					Miss Shot	Go Back 1

C-15. Going to Town.

PROCEDURE

This is a game presenting a learning situation. The pupil first chooses a track. Then he spins the dial or casts a die and proceeds on his track the number of spaces indicated on the dial. (The teacher can help with number recognition.) If the space to which the number advances him contains a word or phrase, he obeys the command. The child take turns, and the one who reaches the end of the track first is declared top player. Players may go down and return on the next track, or they may travel one way only.

Like all other games, after it has served for a "learning" device, it may be used as a social activity.

C-16. *Shell Puppets*

OBJECTIVES
1. To stimulate a desire to express oneself through language.
2. To improve the child's ability to carry on a conversation.
3. To develop oral expression by emphasizing the use of dramatization.
4. To encourage the child to utilize voice and hands to interpret action.
5. To encourage and develop general motor skills.
6. To aid the child to coordinate motor behavior and speech.

MATERIALS
Content in the form of stories or experiences of children for dramatization. Gloves and nut shells on which faces have been painted may be used for puppets. Hollowed-out shells of brazil nuts and pecans are used. Because of the hole in one end, these fit upon the children's fingers. The puppets may be costumed in a number of ways, if desired.

SUBJECT MATTER
Dramatization of familiar stories through oral expression.

PROCEDURE
Stories and experiences are acted out, the children manipulating the glove and nut puppets, making up the dialogue as they go. Begin by selecting stories which have much action and a minimum number of prominent characters. In portraying a puppet be sure that the child speaks in a familiar manner, As "Good morning" or "How do you do?" In a similar manner questions of the teacher's puppet would call for a response: "What is your name?" "How old are you?" "Where do you live?" Other motor actions should be encouraged. If a story is used, be sure that the child

knows the story so that he can express himself in his own words. The teacher may help in formulating the responses the puppet should give and in developing the character.

C-17. *Colored Nail Board*

OBJECTIVES
1. To develop visual perceptual skills.
2. To develop speed and accuracy in activities calling for physical-perceptual coordination.
3. To encourage the use of both hands at the same time when performing activities requiring this.
4. To teach the colors.
5. To aid the child to evaluate his own work for errors and make his own corrections.
6. To develop the ability to attend and to follow directions.

MATERIALS
Peg boards, each about a foot square (a convenient board is a piece of pre-drilled acoustical tile). Most of the boards are painted with green chalk board paint. Others are painted in simple and complicated designs, for example:

	Simple				Complex	
	• • • •	• • • •			• • • •	• • • • Yellow
White	• • • •	• • • • Blue	Orange		• • • •	• • • • Blue
	• • • •	• • • •			• • • •	• • • •
	• • • •	• • • •			• • • •	
	• • • •	• • • •			• • • •	• • • • Green
Red	• • • •	• • • • Green	Red		• • • •	• • • •
	• • • •	• • • •			• • • •	• • • • Red
	• • • •	• • • •			• • • •	• • • •

Numerous roofing nails painted in common colors to match the nail board. The designs may be constructed so that there will be a large range of complexity.

SUBJECT MATTER
Visual recognition of shapes, colors, and positions (positionality).

PROCEDURE
Specific practice should be given in the identification of the common colors by having the child match colored nails with similarly

C-17. Colored Nail Board.

colored areas on the nail board. Next, using both hands, demonstrate how the colored nails are placed on the board. Give the child practice in this. The simple board is used first, and then those more complex in design are introduced later. It is suggested that use of this device be deferred until a child can match colors.

C-18. *Picture Word Books*

OBJECTIVES

1. To aid the child to recognize and identify words that refer to the immediate environment of the child.

2. To aid the child to pronounce words correctly.
3. To introduce, and give practice in writing in manuscript form.
4. To aid the child to recognize words as a unit (whole) and not as individual letters.
5. To aid the child to utilize the ability to note likenesses and differences.

C-18. Picture Word Book.

MATERIALS

Books, with cardboard backs, displaying pictures of members of a family, a person, parts of a house, etc., and under each, the printed name for the picture. Separate cards containing the words used under each picture are provided.

The first book pertains to the family: father, mother, sister, brother, grandfather and grandmother, aunt, uncle, friends, pets, etc. This is followed by books referring to the child's body: head, eyes, eyelashes, eyebrows and nose, mouth, arms, etc. Other books refer to furniture and equipment of the various rooms in a house, to animals, to clothing, etc.

SUBJECT MATTER

Word recognition and identification; word matching.

PROCEDURE

The teacher selects the relevant pictures to a specific topic, for instance, family, out of magazines and cuts them out. These pictures are put between the plastic sheets of the Picture Word Book without gluing them on the paper. The pertinent word tabs in manuscript are placed below the pictures. The prepared word book is set before the child. The child identifies the picture, names the printed word, takes the identical word card in manuscript out of a line of word cards in front of him and puts it beneath the page of the word book. If it is done correctly, the word card is placed aside. This is continued until the child can identify all the pictures with words and word cards. Difficult words are reviewed separately. After the child is able to match the words along with the pictures for each topic, ask him to identify the words without the pictures.

The next step is to let the child match the tabs in manuscript with word cards in transition and finally with word cards in cursive.

(In a similar manner, the child may be introduced to cursive writing in the following units: (1) *My Body,* (9) *What Are They Doing?* (10) *Fine Food,* and (12) *Numbers.* Assorted cards containing one word each, in manuscript, joined-letter, or cursive forms may be used here.)

(1) *My Body* 24 Cards

Head	arm
eyes	face
eyelashes	ear
eyebrow	hair
forehead	back
nose	elbow
lips	hand
mouth	fingers
teeth	finger nails
tongue	thumb
neck	feet
chin	toes

(2) *Family and Friends* 17 Cards

house	Uncle Bill
father	Aunt Jane

mother

brother

sister, Pat

dog, Brutus

Grandfather Smith

Grandmother

Grandfather Buchtel

Cousin Harriett, Cousin Jack

Neighbor Betty

Neighbor James

teacher

Dr. McGlone

mailman

(3) *Dining Room* 21 Cards

dining table

percolater

chair

cupboard

china closet

dishes

buffet

venetian blinds

water pitcher

cup and saucer

teaspoon

fork

water glass

high chair

serving cart

cream pitcher

silverware

cake knife

soup spoon

knife

salad fork

(4) *Kitchen* 23 Cards

pressure cooker

deep freezer

kitchen table

deepfryer

oven

dishwasher

coffee pot

double boiler

broiler

teakettle

refrigerator

mixmaster

dishrack

stewpan

ladle

waste basket

butcher knife

worktable

cupboard

range

shelf

frying pan

toaster

(5) *Bedroom* 20 Cards

bedroom

flower vase

double bed

cedar chest

vanity dresser

blankets

baby bed

quilts

bedroom slipper

shoe pockets

center table

single bed

baby bag

mattress

portiers drapes

straight back chair

chest of drawers

twin beds

dresser

dressing table

(6) *Utility Room* 20 Cards

drying rack

hammers

furnace

clothes dryer

vacuum sweeper
washing machine
wood saws
flat iron
pinking shears
workshop
mops
carpet sweeper

floor polisher
mangle
water heater
ladder
garden hose
suitcase
sewing machine
ironing board

(7) *Bathroom* 14 Cards

wash basin
shower bath
mirror
soap dish
hair brushes
bathtub
scales

bath mat
shaving brushes
combs
stool
medicine cabinet
towels
toilet articles

(8) *Animals* 28 Cards

moose
elephant
ducks
cat
wild duck
horse
moth
steer
donkey
colt
dog
eagle
cow
sheep

pups
kangaroo
robin
rat
elk
lion
pig
lioness
pheasant
camel
cattle
bulls
monkeys
deer

(9) *What Are They Doing?* 29 Cards

pointing
ironing
drinking
skating
writing
climbing
fishing
playing
dancing
shaving
laughing
painting
dressing
scratching

smoking
yawning
swinging
crawling
sleeping
phoning
skiing
sewing
crying
reading
biting
singing
tasting
washing
smelling

(10) ***Fine Food*** (First Part) 16 Cards

cake	hot dogs
peaches	pie
meatloaf	fruit cake
peas	sausage
baked beans	pancakes
biscuits	toast
catsup	pineapple
muffins	bananas

Fine Food (Second Part) 12 Cards

butter	cookies
soup	chili
carrots	cupcakes
coffee	roast beef
eggs	spaghetti
corn	potatoes

(11) ***Clothing*** (First Part) 16 Cards

overcoat	overshoes
gym shoes	gloves
shorts	ties
bedroom slippers	snowsuit
hat	jackets
blue jeans	skirt
leather jacket	underwear
overalls	shoes

Clothing (Second Part) 14 Cards

belts	sweater
socks	housecoat
slippers	slacksuit
cowboy boots	dress
caps	overshoes
raincoats	handkerchief
shirts	bathrobe

(12) ***Numbers of Objects*** (No. 1-12) 24 Cards

1. airplane	1. bird
2. guns	2. kittens
3. bowls	3. cats
4. shoes	4. wheels
5. drinks	5. pennies
6. sandwiches	6. boys
7. hats	7. balls
8. shoes	8. cookies
9. girls	9. piles
10. fish	10. babies
11. watches	11. ties
12. slices	12. gloves

(13) **Dining Room** (Second Part) 24 Cards

table lamp	arm chair
floor lamp	dish
piano	rugs
secretary	carpet
grandfather clock	couch
telephone	staircase
coffee table	television
curtains	bookcase
chandelier	typewriter
fireplace	radio
firescreen	living room
kneehole desk	clock

C-19. *Word Matching Cards*

OBJECTIVES

1. To build the child's vocabulary in terms of identification, meaning, and pronunciation.
2. To aid the child to identify the words when they are written in print, manuscript, or cursive form.
3. To develop the pupil's ability to attend over a prolonged span.

MATERIALS

Cards made of lacquered Bristol board pasted on small masonite blocks. They vary in size from small (approximately $2'' \times 3''$) to large ($4'' \times 6''$), and contain words in pairs printed in manuscript and the same words in cursive letters.

SUBJECT MATTER

Recognition, identification, and pronunciation of words.

PROCEDURE

A box containing the word cards mentioned above is emptied in front of the child. He is encouraged to find two like words in manuscript. After the child has matched the words, he is asked to match the manuscript and cursive forms of the same word. (This can be very advanced work and is not introduced until the child takes cursive writing as a subject.)

C-20. *Word Racks*

OBJECTIVES

1. To aid in the development of a meaningful vocabulary.

2. To encourage word recognition.
3. To acquaint the child with the process of building from simple elements to complex combinations.
4. To develop perception, manual dexterity, and motor coordination.

MATERIALS
A rack constructed on the fence, so as to accommodate cards of masonite measuring approximately 4″ × 4½″ which may be slid back and forth on a *horizontal plane*. They may be inserted or removed from the rack by sliding them on or off.

SUBJECT MATTER
Word recognition, construction and vocabulary.

PROCEDURE
This is simply an outdoor version of the regular word rack. The teacher places a masonite card bearing two letters (such as AN) on the rack. Other pieces bearing single letters are in a rack above. The teacher tells the child to take one of the single letter pieces from the upper rack and put it with the cards in the lower rack to make a word. He may place his selection either to the right or the left of the two letters to complete a word. This is an activity subject to many variations, depending on the teacher's ingenuity. More advanced pupils can make original words for the other children to recognize and name.

C-21. *Sentence Building Frame*

OBJECTIVES
1. To develop the child's ability in tasks requiring visual perception.
2. To aid in the development of the laterality (left-right) concept.
3. To aid in the development of the directionality (position) concept.
4. To increase the child's reading vocabulary.
5. To aid the child to note similarities and differences in visual material.
6. To teach the child to read verbatim.

MATERIALS

Six pieces of masonite (hereafter referred to as "pages"), 6″ × 9″ × ¼″. Five of these have five sentences printed on each side, making ten printed pages, numbered 1 to 10. There are ten boxes, also numbered 1 to 10, containing pieces of masonite on which are printed single words which exactly duplicate the words of the sentences on each page. The sixth 6″ × 9″ board has five slots 1″ high the length of the board. A rack is provided to hold the printed page in place.

SUBJECT MATTER

Word meaning, sentence building.

PROCEDURE

In the rack before the pupil, the teacher places a printed page and beside it she places the box which corresponds to it. The slotted page is placed before the child, and the teacher begins by finding the first word of the first sentence, and fitting it into the slot. The pupil is asked to find the next word.

C-22. *Story Telling*

OBJECTIVES

1. To aid the child to develop a word recognition vocabulary.
2. To aid the child to improve his language facility.
3. To improve the child's listening ability.
4. To strengthen the child's ability to attend to verbal stimuli in general (concentration).

MATERIALS

Printed stories, based on everyday experiences, in which the nouns are omitted. Small cards containing nouns which are used to fill in the blanks of the story.

SUBJECT MATTER

Word recognition, sentence construction, ear training.

PROCEDURE

The word cards are dealt out one at a time to the children, face down, until the cards are exhausted. The teacher reads the story and pauses where the break in the script occurs. The first pupil turns up a noun card and pronounces it, and the teacher continues to the next break in the script. Then the next pupil in rotation turns over a noun card from his set and pronounces it. Since the noun cards turned up may be entirely irrelevant to the text the story becomes very funny sometimes, and since the noun is more often than not entirely out of context, the child cannot rely on context to help in pronouncing the word.

C-23. *Word Sequence Book*

OBJECTIVES
1. To develop the ability to identify and recognize words.
2. To develop the ability to build up words into sentences or phrases.
3. To aid the child in making a transition from manuscript to cursive writing.
4. To develop the ability to note likenesses and differences.
5. To develop abilities involving laterality and directionality.
6. To develop the ability to attend to verbal stimuli.

MATERIALS
A story book formed by several cardboard pages held together with a spiral plastic binding. The words of the story are printed in manuscript form.

In addition, there are two sets of small squares of masonite (approximately $1'' \times 1''$) with words printed on them, one set in manuscript form and the other set in cursive. These words are the same size as the words printed in the story in the book. The word squares for each story are placed in two separate boxes, one for the cursive and one for the manuscript words.

SUBJECT MATTER
Identification and application of words.

PROCEDURE
The manuscript form of the word is used at first. The child first identifies the words in the book. He covers each word with the small masonite square carrying the same word. Eventually, through practice, the pupil perceives each word as a unit, can identify it, and can recognize it in a sentence. The squares are then eliminated and the child begins to read the words printed

in the story book. Begin by using the word cards in the manuscript form. After the child develops some skill with the manuscript form the cursive form cards may be introduced.

C-24. *Number Identification*

OBJECTIVES
1. To aid the child to recognize and identify numbers.
2. To aid the child to note similarities and differences through matching exercises.
3. To aid the child to develop manual dexterity with stress on finger manipulative skills.
4. To develop the ability to attend.

MATERIALS
Several boxes, each containing sets of identical lower Arabic numbers (1-20) on cards.

SUBJECT MATTER
Recognition and identification (lower numbers).

PROCEDURE
A pupil takes two sets of cards and matches them. After the child has matched the cards, he may need practice in recognizing and identifying the numbers and their order. A game can be played with these cards. Distribute some numbers to each child, then flash a number or call one, and have the child match it from his own numbers if he can.

C-25. *Opaque Projector*

OBJECTIVES
1. To stimulate speech through observation from which discussion and comments may follow.
2. To develop confidence in oral expression e.g., speaking in darkened places.
3. To aid the child to perceive objects presented visually.
4. To aid the child to note foreground and background.
5. To aid the child to discriminate between objects presented visually.
6. To aid the child to select single objects from among other objects presented visually.

7. To integrate visual aids with other areas of instruction such as science, social studies, arts, numbers, and reading (vocabulary development).
8. To illustrate stories from children's books, from children's and popular magazines, and other sources.
9. To stimulate interest in current events and unusual experiences.
10. To aid the child to review the content of a discussion by means of visual aids.

MATERIALS
Opaque projector; suitable materials for projection found in magazines, etc.

SUBJECT MATTER
Visual and auditory stimulation and discrimination.

PROCEDURE
Colored pictures are cut from magazine and placed, if large, upon the sheets of a loose leaf note book. Smaller pictures are glued to stiff cardboard cut to uniform size of 4" × 6". These pictures are grouped according to a "main topic," ranging from simple to complex.

There are several pictures (6 to 10) in each pack which relate to the "main topic." The packs of pictures are again graded according to difficulty. Consequently, progressively more difficult questions can be asked according to the ability of the different pupils in the same class.

Different packs are arranged so that pupils can for instance:
1. Locate and name parts of the body upon request,
2. Point out color and name of different clothing garments,
3. Point out known objects and name them,
4. Count items,
5. Respond to questions such as "Do you see a ————?" "Where is ————?" "Who sees a ————?" etc.

The teacher may comment on the pictures when she first shows them in order to give the class a working start. Gradually, the teacher introduces pictured scenes from which more complicated topics may be discussed, as for example: hygiene, holidays, courtesy and safety; or topics such as scratching mosquito bites, eating unauthorized food, petting strange animals etc.

A still more advanced step could be made by asking: "What are they doing?" "Who are they?" "Which one is larger?" . . . "thinner?" . . . "shorter?" . . . "taller?" etc.

C-26. *Singing* and
D-4. *Folk Dancing*

OBJECTIVES

1. To develop the child's ability to perceive rhythm and to sing harmoniously.
2. To develop refined motor skills in the child.
3. To develop perceptual-motor integration in the child.
4. To develop auditory acuity in terms of pitch and volume of sound.
5. To lengthen memory span by recalling auditory material.
6. To provide opportunity to listen to records, and at times interpret the rhythm in action, such as folk dancing.
7. To introduce songs that depict experiences of the child's local environment, and songs in general.
8. To permit the child to learn folk songs that portray life beyond childhood.
9. To provide recreational activities such as play acting, beating time (clapping, saddle rocking, etc.) and singing in small groups.
10. To permit and encourage interaction in a group situation.
11. To provide an opportunity for intensive social interaction.
12. To impress upon the child the importance of interdependence in a group situation.
13. To develop the concept that organized activities can be fun.

MATERIALS

The selections for singing may be classified under the following areas:
1. The early adult and Stephen Foster's folk songs.
2. Spiritual songs: holiday songs and Negro spirituals.
3. Popular songs.

4. Patriotic songs.
5. Action songs.
6. Story songs.

D-4. Folk Dancing.

Subject Matter

Expression through rhythm; auditory discrimination, development of musical repertoire, development of memory span.

Procedure

1. The children sing in groups. The songs are selected according to interest and the season.
2. In action songs, to develop rhythm, the children beat time by clapping or saddle rocking and other reactions of a physical nature.
3. The words of the songs are taught, but many children with speech difficulties are not able to pronounce distinctly. The chief purpose is that the children react and take an active part during the singing period.
4. At times one child alone, or several pupils are called upon to lead and direct a part of the song.
5. Folk dances of various nations are also an essential part of the music program. This develops the child's reaction to rhythm in his body motions, noting and interpreting different steps.

Some Samples of Singing Activities

1. Name the tune: A pupil is designated, and tries to name the tune being played. If he fails, another child tries. Pupils who recognize the tune raise their hands.

2. Rhythm: Clapping hands. Variations are saddle rocking, clapping thighs with hands, foot stamping.

3. Color name recognition: What color is in this song? The child who recognizes it raises his hand and names the color. Examples: *Green* Sleeves, *Brown* Eyes, and *White* Christmas.

4. Name recognition: What is the person's name? The tune is played and a pupil may name the following, for example: Danny Boy, John Peel, Jimmy Crack Corn, or Waltzing Matilda.

5. Songs referring to nature: What animal? Cottontail, dog, donkey, for example. What bird? Turkey, mocking bird, woodpecker, for example. What flower? Coral bells, lilacs, for example.

6. Pupils sing a verse when they have been designated to do so, for example: *Ain't Goin' to Rain, Army Song, Polly Wolly Doodle, Walking Cane.*

7. Novelty songs with repetitions: *Alouette, John Brown, Today is Monday, Schnitzel Bank, Ain't Goin to Grieve,* for example.

8. Singing games and dances:*

*See Bancroft (1); Pearl (33), and Shaw (42, 43).

a. Hansel and Gretel	j. Waltz Promenade
b. Little Princess	k. Little Man in a Fix
c. Burgermeister	l. Hello My Lover
d. Skip to My Lou	m. Lot 1st Tot
e. Chiapinecas	n. Seven Jumps
f. Blackberry Quadrille	o. Cschbogar
g. Paul Jones	p. Cotton Eyed Joe
h. Cattle Song	q. English and Roman Soldiers
i. Ace of Diamonds	r. Norwegian Mountain March

Folk dances (arranged according to difficulty)

1. Roman and English Soldiers	10. Rye Waltz
2. Hello My Lover	11. Varvouvane
3. Seven Jumps	12. Cattle Song
4. Little Princess	13. Cotton Eyed Joe
5. Cschbogar	14. Virginia Reel
6. Lot 1st Tot	15. Ace of Diamonds
7. Chiapinecas	16. Blackberry Quadrille
8. Little Man in a Fix	17. Norwegian Mountain
9. Tandem Schotische	March

C-27. *Spelling Racks*

OBJECTIVES

1. To develop the ability to note composition of words.
2. To develop the ability to build up small elements into larger units.
3. To aid the child to note relationships between elements in word construction.
4. To develop syllabication and phonetic analysis.

MATERIALS

Several boxes of cards on which are printed syllables (see examples which follow) and consonants. These are printed in lower case letters.

A slotted rack for holding syllable, with space on either side to slide in additional letters.

SUBJECT MATTER

Spelling.

PROCEDURE

The children form words by combining syllables and consonants on the rack. The children would probably like it better if you called the art of "spelling" the art of "making words." A useful and entertaining spelling game can be made of the **Ferris Wheel C-34** by using letters instead of numbers. A child can make more words than are to be found in the lists by adding one letter as a prefix and one as a suffix, and by using more of the letters.

Examples:

        1. AM . . . add H—ham . . . add P—hamp
        2. AM . . . add R—ram . . . add P—ramp
        3. AM . . . add D—dam . . . add P—damp
        4. AM . . . add L—lam . . . add P—lamp

As the child progresses, begin to emphasize the pronunciation of the letter, i.e., the letter "b" is sounded phonetically.

MATERIALS: Examples

Box 1 (7 pieces)	Box 2 (11 pieces)	Box 3 (6 pieces)
-AM	-AT	-ED
ham	rat	ned

ram	bat	ted
pam	hat	wed
dam	mat	fed
jam	oat	bed
tam	fat	
	cat	
	pat	
	sat	
	tat	

Box 4 (7 pieces)	Box 5 (11 pieces)	Box 6 (9 pieces)
-EN	-ET	-IN
ten	wet	gin
ben	pet	fin
pen	jet	bin
den	set	sin
men	met	din
hen	let	win
	bet	kin
	get	pin
	vet	
	net	

Box 7 (11 pieces)	Box 8 (10 pieces)	Box 9 (11 pieces)
-IT	-OB	-OT
lit	sob	hot
kit	rob	cot
tit	gob	tot
bit	fob	jot
fit	cob	not
mit	mob	rot
wit	job	pot
pit	bob	dot
hit	nob	lot
sit		got

Box 10 (8 pieces)	Box 11 (10 pieces)	Box 12 (8 pieces)
-UB	-UN	-UST
sub	hun	rust
rub	dun	lust
hub	sun	must
cub	run	just
pub	fun	dust
tub	bun	bust
bub	gun	gust
	nun	
	pun	

Box 13 (8 pieces)	Box 14 (8 pieces)	Box 15 (11 pieces)
-UT	-OG	-AR
put	dog	bar

cut	jog	car
hut	fog	ear
but	bog	far
tut	log	jar
mut	cog	mar
rut	hog	oar
		par
		tar
		war

Box 16 (6 pieces)	Box 17 (57 pieces)		Box 18 (10 pieces)
-EA	-EA-		-AD
yea	bead	beak	bad
sea	beam	bean	cad
tea	bear	dead	dad
bea	deaf	deal	fad
pea	dean	dear	had
	fear	feat	lad
	gear	head	mad
	heal	heap	pad
	hear	heat	sad
	lead	leaf	
	leak	lean	
	leap	mead	
	meal	mean	
	meat	near	
	neat	peak	
	peas	pear	
	real	read	
	ream	reap	
	rear	seal	
	seam	sear	
	seas	seat	
	teak	teal	
	team	tear	
	teas	teat	
	veal	weak	
	weak	wear	
	year	yeas	
	zeal	beat	

Box 19 (12 pieces)	Box 29 (9 pieces)	Box 21 (10 pieces)
-AN	BA-	CO-
ban	ball	cob
can	bad	cod
dan	bag	cog
fan	bam	con
man	bar	coo
nan	ban	cop
pan	bay	cot

ran	bat	cow
tan		coy
van		
wan		

Box 22 (47 pieces)
-EE-

beef	beer
beet	deed
deem	deep
deer	feed
feel	feet
heed	heel
jeep	jeer
keel	keen
keep	leek
leer	meek
meet	need
peek	peel
peep	peer
reed	reef
reek	reel
see	seek
seen	seem
seep	seer
tee	teem
teen	teeth
wee	weed
week	ween
weep	seed

C-28. *Hoopla Ball*

OBJECTIVES

1. To improve manual skills and bodily coordination.
2. To develop the ability to respond to kinesthetic cues.
3. To develop physical-perceptual integrational skills.
4. To provide large muscle activity for total body adjustment.
5. To develop directionality (proprioceptive cues) in the child.
6. To provide an exercise requiring rapid bodily responses.
7. To provide an opportunity to compete and cooperate in a group situation.

MATERIALS

Several sticks about one yard in length with a cross piece at one end, varying from 6″ to 10″ across. Some, of wood, are straight, but other cross pieces are made of metal which may be bent to a desired arc. Volley balls, or other soft balls are used, the playing field may be gym floor or level area out of doors.

SUBJECT MATTER
Gross muscle activity; hand, arm and body coordination.

PROCEDURE
The game may be played individually, or in small groups, either indoors or out of doors.

In the beginning, the younger pupils push a large ball across the floor or playing field with a stick having a curved cross member (the curve makes it easier to control the direction of the ball). After they have learned to control the direction of the ball, they are given sticks with straight cross pieces, and later they play with smaller balls. Eventually, obstacles are put in the way of the balls, to increase the difficulty according to the growth of skill.

C-29. *Word Development*

OBJECTIVES
1. To provide the child with an opportunity to develop word facility, through a sequential build up.
2. To aid the child to note relationship between concrete and abstract forms.
3. To aid the child to make the transition from manuscript to cursive writing.

MATERIALS
Picture books, as described in C-18, also see above. Small word cards (approximate size $1\frac{1}{4}'' \times 1\frac{1}{2}'' \times \frac{1}{4}''$) made out of masonite and covered with shellac. The print on each word card is the exact size of the print under the pictured items. The assorted cards contain either manuscript, joined letter, or cursive letter forms of print.

SUBJECT MATTER
Writing, word-phrase and sentence building.

PROCEDURE
The word cards are presented to the child as models to reproduce

from. In the first lessons, only the manuscript forms of the letters are introduced. When the child can read and write the manuscript letters, the jointed letter forms are presented. Later, the child is encouraged to note how the manuscript letters are joined to form the words in cursive form.

EXAMPLES:

Manuscript

My house
My new house
My big new house
My big house is new
My new house is big
This is my big new house

Joined Letters

My house
My new house
My big new house
My big house is new
My new house is big
This is my big new house

Cursive Letters

My house
My new house
My big new house
My big house is new
My new house is big
This is my big new house

C-29. Word Development.

C-30. *Number Sequence Board*

OBJECTIVES

1. To introduce a sequence of counting.
2. To provide a visual method of teaching numbers.
3. To demonstrate the value of numbers by utilizing concrete objects.
4. To hold the place in counting to enable a pupil to continue if interrupted by distraction.

C-30. Number Sequence Board.

MATERIALS

The Sequence Board is of plywood $10'' \times 21\frac{1}{2}''$ and $\frac{1}{2}''$ thick, divided and numbered as illustrated. In each of the spaces numbered 1 through 10, holes are drilled: one in the space marked *1;* two in the *2* space, etc.

Ten pieces of masonite that fit loosely in each of the center divisions. One side of each is yellow and they are numbered from 1 through 9. The other side is blank. The only exception is number 0 which has on its reverse side a tag marked *5.*

Additional equipment are plastic boxes containing roofing nails and other small objects such as steel washers, steel nuts, buttons, pebbles, etc.

SUBJECT MATTER

Counting in sequence.

PROCEDURE

Teach the child to place a nail in the hole under the *1* and count it aloud. Then put one nail under the *2* and count the *1* and *2* while touching each with a finger. Continue this manner of using only one nail under each symbol. Start at *1* with every counting. The next step is the filling of all the holes under a given number while counting. When familiar with *10*, introduce the numbers from *11* to *20* on the upper side of the board by placing the designated number of objects upon the proper numeral. Always start at *1* by placing one object in the proper space, and use each space in sequence through *20*. Count back by removing each object in turn, starting at *1* and putting objects in box.

The yellow tags, numbered from *0* to *9*, are used by placing them to the left of the lower row of numbers to make numbers in the tens.

Example:

2 is moved along the board with pauses to make the *20* series. That is, to make *21, 22,* and *23,* etc., place or hold the piece *2* beside numbers *1, 2, 3,* etc. When *29* is reached, a yellow *3* is placed on the *1* in *10*. In this manner, continue until *99* is reached. Then put the *0* tag to the right of the *10*.

The numbers in the middle, from *10* through *55,* are used to prepare the pupils for telling time by learning to count by *5*'s.

Example:

Cover all the numbers of the middle row, except *10*, with the blank reverse side of the yellow series; cover *10* with the reverse side of number *0* which shows a *5*. Have children read this *5*. Then remove it and have them read the *10* which was covered. Next remove the cover of *15* and place it over *10*. Continue in this manner by having the children read, in unison, the single number that is exposed.

OTHER ACTIVITIES

The yellow number pieces can be placed in sequence order in rows horizontally and perpendicularly.

Be sure that the horizontal rows start with the lowest number at the left and that the lowest numbers start the perpendicular rows at the bottom and work up in value.

As the holes for the nails in the lower row are drilled through the board, the board can be turned over for another application.

Let the student put the proper number of nails in a given space, for example: three roofing nails in the three holes. Then have the pupil place the proper yellow tag under these nails, in our case the tag with the *3*.

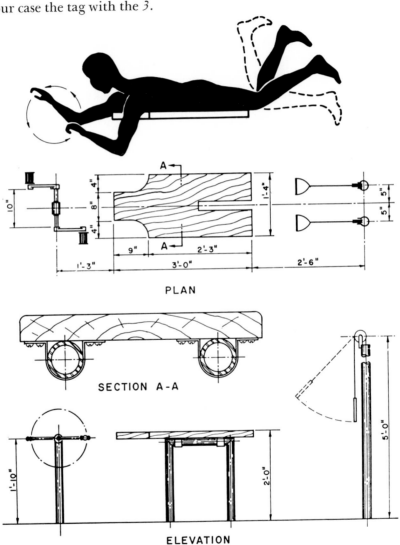

PLAN

SECTION A-A

ELEVATION

SWIM EXERCISE TABLE

C-31. Swimming Tables.

C-31. *Swimming Tables*

OBJECTIVES

1. To develop the child's awareness of kinesthetic, tactile, and proprioceptive cues.
2. To aid in the development of physical-perceptual integration.
3. To aid in the development of body (and postural) adjustment.
4. To develop the child's ability to swim.

MATERIALS

See illustration. Swimming tables are made out of wood, pipe, bolts, straps, pulley wheels, rope, bicycle pedal housing, cement, 4 weights and cans filled with cement. At one end of the table the bicycle pedals are fastened, one for each arm. At the other end weights are placed, which are activated with the legs.

SUBJECT MATTER

Swimming training; bodily adjustment, motor-coordination.

PROCEDURE

The child lies on his stomach on the swimming table. His thighs are strapped down if necessary. He kicks his legs alternately with his feet in the stirrups.

Next, he learns to use his arms, turning the two bicycle pedals in front of him without moving his legs. After he can use his legs and arms independently in swimming movements, he learns to use legs and arms simultaneously as in swimming.

C-32a. *Writing I (Exercises for "Writing Readiness")*

GENERAL REMARKS

Penmanship requirements have been developed for normal pupils who have fine motor dexterity. Children who are mentally subnormal have been found to need writing exercises that guide and help them even on drills that are very simple. Most of the examples of practice drills are based upon drawn figures which introduce lines and curves from the simple form to the complex, and which, finally, combine line and curve in one figure.

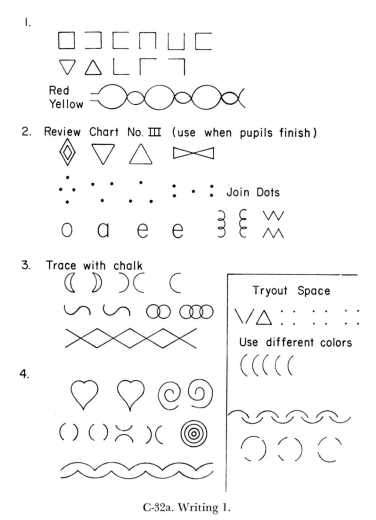

C-32a. Writing 1.

OBJECTIVES

1. To develop manual dexterity in exercises that aid writing.
2. To develop perceptual-motor integration.
3. To introduce variations of line and circle exercises which are essential in letter formation.
4. To develop the ability to trace straight lines and curves.
5. To improve the ability to color and outline.

5. Complete circles — Use curve lines

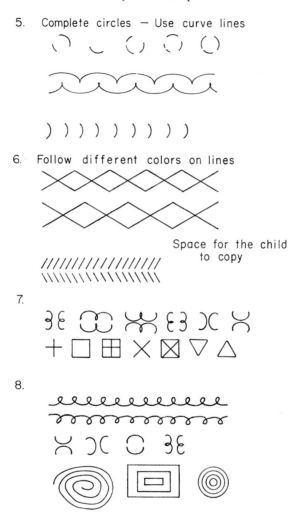

6. Follow different colors on lines

Space for the child to copy

7.

8.

MATERIALS

Three sets of rectangular masonite boards $24'' \times 36'' \times \frac{1}{8}''$ on which have been painted simple lines, curves and geometric forms of graduated difficulty. Each set is painted a distinctive color. Full directions for their use are printed on the back of each board.

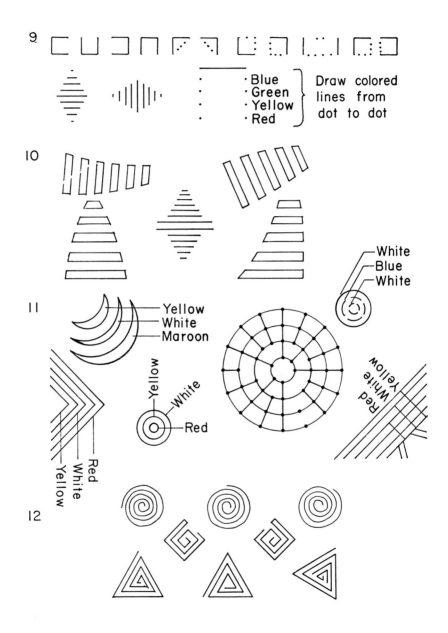

SUBJECT MATTER

Manual dexterity and coordination; writing readiness.

PROCEDURE

The children are encouraged to trace, and in some cases to finish the square, rectangular and circular figures with chalk. The exercises are developed in terms of difficulty, introducing the straight line first, and gradually the simple to complex curves. As the children learn to trace, colors are presented by asking the children to follow specific lines with colored chalk.

EXAMPLES OF TEACHING STEPS: (see illustrations 1-12 above)

1. Follow "wave lines" and complete triangles and squares.
2. Follow arcs and complete circles.
3. Complete squares from triangles. Follow graduating lines horizontally and perpendicularly and copy them.
4. Cover the "slanting-to-the-right" lines with chalk, and then follow the remaining jagged line with a different color. Follow the next row of jagged lines with other colors. Next make Row 1 design on Row 2 (superimposed). In the empty space in the middle, draw freehand, any of the four exercises on this board.
5. Follow the lines on all figures from the outside in; later, inside out.
6. Follow reverse curves and small rectangles and circles of different colors.
7. Follow lines of angles, then fill them in, and where possible, use different colors.
   Then unite dots to form the figures just below the two lines.

C-32b. *Writing II (Use of Pictures for "Writing Readiness")*

OBJECTIVES

1. To improve manual dexterity.
2. To aid the child to note details in terms of the figures and colors in the pictures.
3. To develop speed and accuracy in tasks requiring manual dexterity.
4. To develop a higher level of physical-perceptual coordination.
5. To increase attention and interest for completion of the task.

Writing IIb.

MATERIALS

Two sets of rectangular masonite boards $15'' \times 20'' \times \frac{1}{8}''$ on which are drawn pictures of varying difficulty. The color of the outlined picture indicates the color to be used in the tracing. The pictures are of items the child knows from every day life, such as animals, children, trains, etc. (These may be copied from ordinary drawing books available in dime and drug stores.)

Set 2 varies from Set 1 in that it has finer detail.

SUBJECT MATTER

Tracing and coloring.

PROCEDURE

Let the children first follow or trace lines on Set. 1. On Set 2, the pupils note finer details, requiring finer muscular coordination and more attention in the selection of colors. The pictures must be traced and filled in with the proper colors as indicated by the outlines.

C-32. Writing IIb.

C-32c. *Writing III (Print Manuscript and Cursive Writing)*

MATERIALS

Rectangular boards 24″ × 36″ × $\frac{1}{8}$″, painted with green chalkboard finish, on which signs and letters are written as illustrated on the preceding pages.

PROCEDURE

1. Instruct the pupils to follow the lines with chalk; encourage the development of a light touch.
2. Know the letter *o*, which is a circle; *c* is part of a circle; *e* is nearly a circle, but has a cross-mark; *a* is a circle with a tail.
3. Know that several letters have a circle *o* as one of its parts, such as *d, b, p, q,* and *g* in the lower case.
4. Trace the *o*'s, *c*'s, *e*'s, and *a*'s on the samples on the board. (After the child can trace *o*, he is asked to make *o*'s in the space provided beneath the sample. In like manner, the child first

traces *c*'s, *e*'s and *a*'s on the board. After he gains proficiency, he writes these letters in the space provided below the samples.)

5. Add the handle that determines what the letter will be. Exercise with *o*'s first. On each *o, o, o, o,* put handles on the right, pointing up to make *d,* or on the left, pointing up, to make *b.* Put handles on the lower left side, pointing down to make *p,* and a handle on the right side to make *q.* By adding a curve on the handle *q* becomes a *g.*

6. Introduce the group of letters which are open at the top, like *u, y, v,* and *w,* following the same development procedure as in the *circle* letters.

7. Introduce letters which are open at the bottom as *h, n,* and *m.*

After the child has learned to trace the letters well, have him write the letters on the spaces below the letters.

C-33. *Counting Pans*

OBJECTIVES

1. To strengthen the ability to recognize and identify numbers.
2. To enlarge number concepts in the child.
3. To aid the child to note a connection between the concrete object and the abstract symbol which represents it.
4. To develop the child's ability to attend.

MATERIALS

The Counting Pans consist of standard muffin pans of heavy tinware. Each end of the pan is screwed to wooden strips $1\frac{1}{2}''$ wide, $\frac{1}{2}''$ thick, and 12″ long. These strips extend 1″ beyond the pans to prevent tipping.

In addition to the pans there are 24 or more discs of heavy cardboard. Each disc is $1\frac{3}{4}''$ in diameter and bears on both sides a number from 1 to 20. (There is a duplication of the smaller numbers.)

There are also twelve transparent plastic boxes, each about $2\frac{1}{2}'' \times 3\frac{3}{4}'' \times 1\frac{1}{2}''$ containing small everyday items such as screws, buttons, lima beans, washers, pebbles, etc. The contents are marked in manuscript or print on backs and fronts of the plastic boxes. There are also up to fifty tabs made of heavy cardboard, $\frac{3}{4}'' \times 2\frac{1}{2}''$ each, marked the same way as the plastic boxes.

SUBJECT MATTER

Counting, through recognition and identification of words and numbers.

C-33 Counting Pans.

PROCEDURE

Place one disc and one tab in the bottom of each section of the muffin pan. Then, proceeding one section at a time, have the child say the number on the disc, and let him read the name of the object on the tab. The child selects the plastic box of objects bearing the same name as that on the tab and counts the required number of objects into the proper section of the pan. (If necessary use the sequence board.) Proceed in this fashion until all the divisions are filled. Finally, the teacher checks the pans for the correct response. She changes the numbers discs and the objects tabs in each pan, and the child repeats the procedure until all discs and tabs have been introduced.

C-34. *Ferris Wheel*

OBJECTIVES
1. To aid the child to recognize visual symbols.
2. To develop physical-perceptual integration in the child.
3. To develop beginning number concepts.
4. To aid the child to attend to tasks requiring attention and concentration.

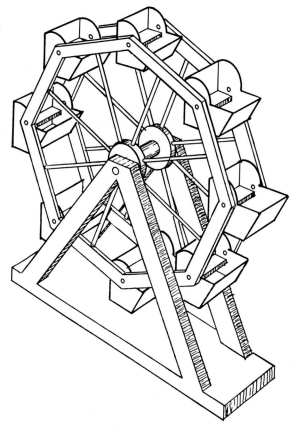

C-34. Ferris Wheel.

5. To aid the child to note similarities and differences.
6. To aid the child to follow directions.

MATERIALS
A miniature ferris wheel, similar to those used in amusement parks is used. On the outside, between the seats, a space is provided on which numbers are written. Plastic or wooden counters.

SUBJECT MATTER
Recognition of numbers and number names.

PROCEDURE
Several children play this as a game. The teacher writes those numbers which she particularly wants to teach on the provided space. Then she gives each child a card with one of those numbers painted on it. She writes the name and relevant number of each participating child on the blackboard. The teacher or a pupil spins the wheel. When the wheel stops, the number which shows between the two supports of the wheel is the winning number. The child identified with this number gains one chip. The game is continued until every pupil has had at least one chance. The top player is the one with the most chips when period ends.

C-35. *Dominoes with Pictures and/or Arabic Numbers*

OBJECTIVES
1. To aid the child to recognize printed numbers.
2. To aid the child to note similarities and differences in forms.
3. To develop physical-perceptual skills through matching exercises.
4. To develop the ability to attend to tasks requiring attention and concentration.

MATERIALS
Cards the size and shape of dominoes, some with two pictures

EXAMPLES: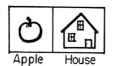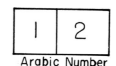

C-35. Dominoes with pictures and/or Arabic numbers.

on each side, some with two Arabic numbers printed on each side. The latter are white on one side, blue on the other. The white sides are numbered 1-6; the blue sides, 7-12.

SUBJECT MATTER
Recognition and matching of numbers and symbols.

PROCEDURE
The children are first introduced to the picture domino cards. Ask them to match the pictures at each end of the card by placing them next to identical pictures on other "dominoes." After the child has learned to place the pictures together, the domino cards with Arabic numbers are introduced.

C-36. *Number Casino*

OBJECTIVES
1. To aid the child to recognize and identify number symbols.
2. To aid the child to note similarities and differences through matching exercises.
3. To provide opportunities to follow directions and take turns.

MATERIALS
Small cards made of masonite $2\frac{1}{2}'' \times 3'' \times \frac{1}{2}''$, painted with numbers from 1 through 12. There are two sets, twelve pairs of cards each. One set has a green background, the other set has black background.

SUBJECT MATTER
Recognition and identification of number symbols.

PROCEDURE
Each child is given four cards, face down. Also, four cards of the same color are placed face up on the table before the players. The first pupil compares the numbers of the cards he has with the numbers of the cards on the table. If one of his number cards matches a card on the table, he takes this card and the next child has his turn. If the first pupil has no card in his set to match the cards on the table, he has to place one of his cards on the table, face up, and the next child takes his turn. This is continued until

each child has played out his whole set of cards. Then a new set of four is distributed. This goes on until all twelve pairs of cards have been played. The pupil with the most cards wins.

Then another set of a different color can be played. Later, both sets are used with the same procedure as described before but only black can match black or green match green.

C-37. *Fantan*

OBJECTIVES
1. To develop number concepts in the child.
2. To emphasize interaction in a group situation and stimulate social relationships for the child.
3. To develop the ability to attend to verbal stimuli.
4. To aid the child to develop motivation toward academic activities.
5. To develop visual imagery in the child.

MATERIALS
Masonite game board which is rectangular in shape as per example:
Colored plastic chips and
objects such as pebbles, beans, buttons, etc.

1	3
2	4

SUBJECT MATTER
Number recognition and identification.

PROCEDURE
Two or more children can play this game. Each child receives several chips, a different color for each child. The teacher takes a handful of small objects, such as buttons, and places them on the table under a bowl. Each child picks a number on the game board and puts one of his chips on it. The teacher then removes the objects from under the bowl in sets of four, and places them in view until there are only four or less left under the bowl. The number of objects left in the final group determines the winner for that go-around. For instance, if two are left over, the child who placed his chip on "2" of the game board wins all the chips on the board. The child who has the most chips after several games is the winner.

C-38. *Value of Money*

OBJECTIVES
1. To develop arithmetical concepts.
2. To improve the child's ability to handle money.
3. To provide practical experiences in the use of money.
4. To enable the pupil to make computations.
5. To provide experiences stressing the value of money.

C-38. Values of Money.

MATERIALS
Imitation money and real coins: pennies, nickels, dimes, quarters, and half dollars.

SUBJECT MATTER
Quantitative concepts involving money.

PROCEDURE
At first introduce penny and nickel. Put five pennies on the table

with a nickel and have the child note that five pennies equal a nickel. Make a game, and give him the same amount of gum, candy, or a pencil for five pennies as you give him for a nickel. In like manner, present the more advanced money situation such as two nickels equal one dime, etc. (This unit can utilize the opaque projector (C-25) if pictures of familiar commodities can be projected while the unit is carried out.)

C-39. *Table Shuffleboard*

OBJECTIVES
1. To develop a recognition of number symbols.
2. To develop the ability to respond to perceptual cues.
3. To develop space and form perception.
4. To familiarize the child with the essentials of game playing, competition.
5. To develop ability in concentration and attention.
6. To prepare the child for participation in the standard games.

MATERIALS
A small facsimile of a regular shuffle board, painted on top of a table (treated first with chalk-board paint); discs or puck, and a shuffleboard cue. Our shuffleboard is painted on one end of an 8' table, and measures 2'5" from point to base. A line is painted about 14" from the other end, and second and third lines are painted about 22" and 30" from that end.

SUBJECT MATTER
Number recognition, space and form perception, manual manipulation.

PROCEDURE
This game, a variation of regular shuffleboard, is a number teaching device as well as a social game. Into the spaces of the shuffleboard, the teacher writes numbers which she is currently teaching the class, taking care that they are right side up for a child standing at the opposite end of the table from the triangle. Beginners place the puck on the second line and, using the cue, push it sharply forward into a numbered space. The cue is not to follow

the puck beyond the third line. More advanced pupils place the puck at the first line, and the cue must not follow the puck past the second line. Teacher and pupil together add the score which the teacher records with chalk on the table itself.

Beginners must be instructed on the use of the cue and some practice shots should be allowed. Several children play at the same time and may play singles or doubles, as in regular shuffleboard. After a child has gained proficiency in adding his score, the section of the board farthest removed from the point may be filled with a number to be subtracted from totals.

Example:

A pupil may add 1, 3 and 5 = 9. The total is recorded. If the puck then comes to rest on the subtraction space, that number is subtracted. More advanced players are chosen to calculate the scores (using the Number Columns reported under C-33) involving addition and subtraction operations.

C-40. *Number Columns*

OBJECTIVES
1. To develop number concepts in the child.
2. To aid the child to note a step by step build-up of arithmetical understandings.
3. To aid the child, through concrete means, to comprehend abstract symbols.
4. To aid the child to attend to tasks requiring attention and concentration.

MATERIALS

The "Number Columns" (see illustration) consist of 3 dowel rods mounted in an upright fashion on a wooden base. Each dowel rod is 10″ high, $\frac{1}{2}$″ in diameter, and set in the center of a square piece of hardwood $7\frac{1}{2}$″ × $7\frac{1}{2}$″ × 1″.

The first rod indicates units. On it, as 1″ intervals, are painted the numerals one through nine. These are numbered from the bottom up, with "1" in the lowest space and "9" at the top. The second rod, which indicates tens (ten through ninety) and the third, which indicates hundreds (one hundred through nine hundred) are numbered in the same manner.

There are 27 wooden rings, 1″ high, which fit over the dowel rods. Each ring has an outside diameter of $^{15}/_{16}″$ or 1″ and an inside diameter of $^{5}/_{16}″$. The rings for the units column are marked from one through nine, and the rings for tens and hundreds columns are not marked.

For advanced pupils there is a variation of this exercise which is known as *Number Columns Combination*. For this, the 3 columns are mounted on one hardwood block $7\frac{1}{2}″ \times 7\frac{1}{2}″ \times 1″$. The columns for the tens and hundreds are removable for greater flexibility.

C-40. Number Columns.

SUBJECT MATTER
Perception of numbers, number concepts.

PROCEDURE
Using the Problem board (C-7) in combination if desired, the child solves simple arithmetical problems. Using the Unit Column he begins with the addition of number combinations to

ten. To find, for instance, the solution for 2 plus 5 the child takes 2 rings out of a box and puts them over the rod of the unit square. When he drops one ring over the rod, the numeral "1" appears just above it. When he drops the second ring on top of the first, the numeral "2" will appear above the ring. Then he counts out five more rings and puts them on top of the first two. In this manner, as each successive ring is added, the total number of rings on the rod is indicated. When the student masters the units device the teacher gives problems for the tens in the same manner, follows with tens and units, and finally the hundreds, followed by hundreds, tens and units. By the same process, subtraction, multiplication and division may be introduced.

A supplementary exercise may be found in the Appendix, pages 251-254.

C-41. *Clock Dial*

OBJECTIVES
1. To familiarize the child with Arabic numbers.
2. To improve counting skills.
3. To develop concepts in the child as to time.
4. To develop the ability to read clock face.
5. To develop manual dexterity.

MATERIALS
Clock face with Arabic numbers; a $\frac{1}{4}''$ dowel pin, 2" long, with a suction cup on one end; an hour hand 3" long, painted black on one side; a minute hand $4\frac{1}{2}''$ long. Both hands have a hole in the broad end to fit over the dowel pin.

SUBJECT MATTER
Practice in telling time; knowledge of counting (by fives).

PROCEDURE
The large clock face with the dowel pin in the center, is placed before the children. At first, the hour hand only, black side up, is placed on the dowel. One of the children flicks the hour hand, and the teacher asks a child, "What is the hour?" The children rotate the hand until each is familiar with the hours.

Then the hour hand is removed and the minute hand is substituted. A child flicks the minute hand and the other children note the minutes in terms of *5, 10, 15,* etc., minutes. The process is continued until all are familiar with minutes.

After hours and minutes are reported efficiently and separately, both hands of the clock are used, until the children can recognize and identify the hours and minutes together.

(This can be either a group or individual activity.)

C-42. *Number Book*

OBJECTIVES

1. To develop word recognition ability.
2. To develop number concepts.
3. To aid the child to make transitions from concrete objects to abstract symbols.
4. To aid the child to note similarities and differences among forms and symbols.

MATERIALS

A book displaying pictures of different objects (one to twelve objects each page). The appropriate number symbols and the words for these objects appear on each page.

In addition, small individual cards with print which matches that found in the book, made of $\frac{1}{8}''$ masonite $1'' \times 4''$, with one number symbol and one word printed on each.

Example:

Number and Word	*Number and Word*
1 wheel	7 overshoes
2 boys	8 feet
3 girls	9 scales
4 bulbs	10 beds
5 pipes	11 bottles
6 lighters	12 women

SUBJECT MATTER

Word recognition, number concept development.

PROCEDURE

The teacher shows the pictures in the book with the words and the number symbols written under each picture in manuscript form. She asks the child to name the picture and the number. If he cannot name them the teacher helps the child, perhaps in the following manner: "This is *one wheel.*" She may point to the wheel, to the word for wheel, and the symbol *1.* In like manner, the other pictures and numbers are dealt with.

The teacher encourages the pupils to match the masonite pages with the numbers and words in the book. This provides remedial work for the pupils who need this type of additional help.

C-43. *Thinking Caps*

OBJECTIVES

1. To intensify the child's familiarity with numbers and number concepts.
2. To further develop self-awareness and self-identity.
3. To introduce pleasure in the learning situation.
4. To emphasize interaction in a group situation and stimulate social relationships for the child.

C-43. Thinking Caps.

MATERIALS

Felt caps without visors, or beanies, each bearing a number on the front.

SUBJECT MATTER

Knowledge of numerals (Arabic).

PROCEDURE

Each child receives and wears a numbered cap. To help him become familiar with his number, the teacher devises simple procedures. For instance, she will ask the pupil to show by his fingers the number his cap calls for.

After several sessions, he is given another cap with a different number. However, he is not given a number contingent to the one he had previously because this proves to be confusing for the child.

The Thinking Cap can also be used in connection with the Ferris Wheel, Horse Races and Going to Town (games) where the number on the cap is also assigned to the pupil for the game.

C-44. *Tick-Tack-Toe*

OBJECTIVES

1. To aid the child to develop spatial, directional, and lateral concepts.
2. To develop manual dexterity skills.
3. To develop color discrimination.
4. To develop the concept of order and taking turns.

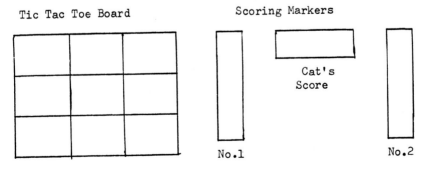

C-44. Tick-Tack-Toe.

MATERIALS

Paint a tick-tack-toe board on the top of a table or on a masonite board, as shown. As pawns, use salve boxes, or wooden blocks in sets of four different colors. In order to score the results of the game, scoring markers may be drawn as illustrated.

SUBJECT MATTER

Color discrimination in a spatial setting.

PROCEDURE

Two pupils play the game, taking turns. The aim, as in tick-tack-toe, is to place three pawns in a row, either vertically, horizontally or diagonally. The child who first completes a row of three pawns receives credit for that game.

C-45. *Manuscript and Cursive Writing*

OBJECTIVES

1. To introduce cursive writing.
2. To associate manuscript and cursive writing.
3. To demonstrate how manuscript writing is closely related to script by joining the manuscript letters to form script letters in writing words.
4. To facilitate the transition from manuscript to cursive writing.

MATERIALS

Books with words written in manuscript (in manuscript letters which are joined with fine lines) and in cursive writing (see examples). Boards and tables.

SUBJECT MATTER

Manuscript and cursive writing.

PROCEDURE

At first the pupils learn to identify the words and statements that are written with manuscript letters. When they are able to read these words in manuscript form, the words in joined-manuscript letters are introduced and identified. After practice, the words

	MANUSCRIPT	JOINED LETTERS	CURSIVE
Initial:	fin	*fin*	*fin*
	bin	*bin*	*bin*
	din	*din*	*din*
	pan	*pan*	*pan*
	nan	*nan*	*nan*
	van	*van*	*van*
	can	*can*	*can*
	ran	*ran*	*ran*
	man	*man*	*man*
	fan	*fan*	*fan*
Body:	nose	*nose*	*nose*
	lips	*lips*	*lips*
	mouth	*mouth*	*mouth*
	teeth	*teeth*	*teeth*
	tongue	*tongue*	*tongue*
	neck	*neck*	*neck*
	chin	*chin*	*chin*
	ear	*ear*	*ear*
	hair	*hair*	*hair*
Numbers:	one	*one*	*one*
	two	*two*	*two*
	three	*three*	*three*
	four	*four*	*four*
	five	*five*	*five*
	six	*six*	*six*
	seven	*seven*	*seven*
	eight	*eight*	*eight*
	nine	*nine*	*nine*
	ten	*ten*	*ten*

C-45. Manuscript and Cursive Writing.

written in cursive form are introduced. For additional practice, brief phrases are presented in both manuscript, joined letter, as well as in cursive forms.

C-46. *Paper Beads*

OBJECTIVES
1. To develop higher skills in manual dexterity.
2. To develop physical-perceptual skills.
3. To develop the child's interest in artistic activities.

MATERIALS
Four tapered plastic templates in pennant form $\frac{1}{2}'' \times 9''$, $\frac{3}{4}'' \times 10\frac{1}{2}''$, $1'' \times 13''$, and $2'' \times 14''$. Wallpaper of different colors and small patterns. Thick paste, cotter pins, lacquer.

SUBJECT MATTER
Manual dexterity.

PROCEDURE
Template is placed upon the back of a sheet of wallpaper and the child marks around it with a pencil after which he cuts it out with scissors. To form the paper beads, he places the wide end in the split of a cotterpin and rolls it toward the point after he has spread the back side with thick paste. He removes the bead by pushing it off of the pin and places a pencil in the hole to hold the bead while painting it with clear lacquer. When stringing beads they may be weighted by using glass beads as spacers.

Marking may be done by one pupil, pasting by another and cutting by still another, but jobs should be rotated when possible.

C-47. *Stepping Blocks*

OBJECTIVES
1. To provide opportunities through exercises involving maintenance of equilibrium.
2. To develop balance.
3. To develop posture.
4. To develop concepts and skills in directionality and laterality.
5. To develop an awareness of one's place in space.

MATERIALS

Set I

Three smooth hardwood blocks 2″ × 4″ × 7″.

Set II

Three blocks of the same measurements as for Set I that have been planed to triangular shape on underside. Block #1 has the point running full length of block. Block #2 has the point across the width. Block #3 has the point running obliquely from left front to right back.

SUBJECT MATTER

Maintenance of equilibrium and postural development.

PROCEDURE

For Set I and in similar way for Set II:

Stand with each foot on a block with feet side by side and 6″ apart. Place the third block a length ahead of the right foot. Step on it with the right foot, bend over and pick up the extra block with the right hand and place it a length ahead of the left foot.

Repeat this procedure by placing the extra block in front of one foot and then the other.

For Progressive Difficulty:

1. After placing extra block, stand erect, raise both arms straight above head, with elbows and fingers straight and the head well back.
2. Recover extra block by reaching in back with the opposite hand.
3. Combine procedures #1 and #2.
4. Work with only two blocks without touching hands to the floor.
5. Combine procedures #1 and #4.

INTEGRATED PHYSICAL-PERCEPTUAL SKILLS

Units of Instruction

THIS LAST GROUP of units of instruction includes activities which require a comparatively high degree of coordination between motor activities and perceptual processes. Exercises are included here which give practice not only in manual dexterity, but in fairly complicated body movements as well. In addition, some of the exercises contribute to the development of occupational skills, social adaptability and group cooperation.

This material is related to the discussion in Chapter 7.

D-1. *Sweeping Box*

OBJECTIVES
1. To aid in the development of adequate postural adjustment.
2. To aid the pupil in developing appropriate responses to physical-perceptual cues.
3. To develop manual skills through motor activity.
4. To aid the pupil to respond to and control visual and kinesthetic sensations.
5. To aid in the development of laterality and directionality.
6. To aid in the vocational career of the student.

MATERIALS
The sweeping box is a rectangle 33' x 52" inside made of heavy boards framed by a 2" x 4" board. In addition, hard to sweep objects such as marbles, strings, nails, etc. are provided, as well as a broom to sweep with.

SUBJECT MATTER
Physical-perceptual integration, postural adjustment, laterality and directionality.

D-1. Sweeping Box.

PROCEDURE

The pupils stand in the sweeping box, which is placed on the ground or floor. Several objects are placed in the box and the pupils are asked to sweep them along or around various obstacles (baffles) being careful to keep them inside the sweeping box. The teacher encourages and aids the pupils to develop general coordination and good body posture for sweeping.

D-2. *Hop Scotch (and Related Games)*

OBJECTIVES
1. To develop a sense of balance.
2. To develop physical-perceptual integration through physical activities.
3. To provide opportunities through exercises involving maintenance of equilibrium; to aid in the development of bodily adjustment and bodily image.

4. To develop an awareness of kinesthetic, visual, and labyrinthine sensations toward carrying out more complex motor activities.

5. To develop ability to attend and concentrate through physical activities.

MATERIALS

Patterns of various kinds of Hop Scotch are painted on cement walks. Space and positions for the feet are painted to indicate where the feet should be placed, one color for left foot, another for the right foot.

SUBJECT MATTER

Bodily adjustment, physical-perceptual coordination.

Two Foot Hop Scotch

o   o   o   o   o   o   o   o

Start with feet apart o together o apart o together o apart o repeat. The child is instructed to stand with feet on the first pattern, then to jump to the second pattern, placing the feet on the painted positions, and to progress down the walk, with feet alternating from separated pattern to closed position.

One Foot Hop Scotch

Start with left foot, hop forward on left foot as indicated in pattern, then hop to right foot as indicated by pattern, then back to left, reducing to two hops, then one hop as indicated in pattern.

Left foot — ooo   ooo   oo   oo   o   o
Right foot — ooo   ooo   oo   oo   o   o

Turning Hop Scotch

This pattern differs from the others by having an "X" painted between rather widely spaced positions for feet placed together. A curved arrow indicates the direction in which the player is to turn on the "X."

Start o o — X) o o — X) o o etc.

The child begins with feet together. Then he is directed to jump straight forward, placing his feet in the the interspaces of the "X." Then he is to jump and turn 90° in the direction indicated by the arrow, placing his feet in the other interspaces of the same "X." The next jump and 90° turn will face him back towards starting position, and two more jumps will put him in the forward position again (total 360° on the same "X"). He jumps forward and proceeds to the next "X," on which the arrow indicates turning in the opposite direction of that on the first "X."

Cross-over of Legs

Right Foot	R	R	R	R	R	R	
	o	o	o	o	o	o	etc.
Left Foot		o	o	o	o	o	
		L	L	L	L	L	

The child is instructed to start by placing his right foot in the first position and to *walk* forward, swinging the left foot forward and across the right foot to the indicated position, then while standing on the left foot, swinging the right foot forward and across in front of the left foot into the indicated position painted on the walk. When the child is proficient in walking forward, have him walk backward, swinging the feet across in back of the stationary foot. Please note, the exercise is not a "hopping" exercise, but a "walking" exercise.

Waltz Step

Pattern:

		L			L			L		
		o			o			o		
	L		L	L		L	L		L	
Start	o		o	o		o	o		o	etc.
	R		R	R		R	R		R	
		o			o					
		R			R					

The child stands with two feet together. He is instructed to advance the left foot to a position forward and to the left of the standing position, then to step straight forward to the indicated position with the right foot, and finally, to close by placing the left foot beside the right foot. From this position he advances the right foot forward and slightly to the right to the indicated position, then steps straight forward with the left foot, and again closes by bringing the right foot forward to place beside the left foot. The pattern is repeated.

D-3. *Bark Splitting*

OBJECTIVES

1. To stimulate the pupil to see or visualize something familiar to him by associating this with something else in his experience.
2. To encourage the pupil to make use of his imagination.
3. To develop awareness of kinesthetic and tactile sensations toward improvement of motor responses.
4. To develop manual dexterity.
5. To develop an appreciation of the esthetic.
6. To aid in the development of attention and concentration.

MATERIALS

The dry bark from a dead pine tree.

SUBJECT MATTER

Manual dexterity, concept formation development.

PROCEDURE

Give the child a piece of bark and encourage him to pick off small pieces. Tell him to look at the pieces and ask him to tell what he sees in the pieces, such as a person, an animal, a boat, a head, etc. At first he may have difficulty visualizing anything, but with practice, he learns to associate the pieces with familiar things in his environment. At first the teacher finds these pieces, and shows them to the pupils. The children then find probable pieces which they give to the teacher to identify. They develop the ability to find likenesses.

D-4. *Folk Dancing*

This unit is explained in connection with *C-26 Singing.*

D-5. *Roller Skating*

Children of all ages at Laradon Hall participate in roller skating activity.

OBJECTIVES

1. To provide recreational activities by introducing individual and group exercises.
2. To develop bodily agility by means of games that require physical reactions.
3. To promote neuro-muscular awareness of the body and its potentialities of movement.
4. To introduce the pupil to group experiences to develop such traits as consideration for others, industry, and manners.

D-5. Roller Skating.

MATERIALS
Roller skates.

SUBJECT MATTER
Physical (motor) coordination.

PROCEDURE

1. Children of about the same age level skate as a group.
2. All furniture (tables, chairs, benches, etc.) is removed from the gym during skating periods.
3. All pupils skate along the walls in the same direction, in a circular pattern.
4. Music is provided by a record player to teach students rhythm in skating.
5. Simple stunts and duets are practiced.

D-6. *Gymnasium Games*

OBJECTIVES

1. To provide recreational activities by introducing individual and group exercises.
2. To develop bodily control by means of games that require physical reactions.
3. To promote neuro-muscular awareness of the body and its potentialities of movement.
4. To introduce the pupils to group experiences to develop such traits as consideration for others, industry, and manners.
5. To make quick and accurate decisions while under pressure.

MATERIALS

The games should be selected in terms of ability level.

    (a) Individual Stunts
        One-leg Hop, right and left
        Knee Dip
        Ape Walk
        Corkscrew Step
        Push Up
        Sit Up
        Marine Dip
        Wiggle Stick
        Stump Walk
        Rocking Chair
        Stepping Blocks (2 and 3 blocks)
        Toe Hold Jump
        Hopscotch

One Leg Kick (right and left)
Push Back
Egg Roll (right and left)
Wring the Dishrag
Rocking Leg Stretch
Crab Walk
Seal Walk
Arm Pivot Circle (right and left)
(b) Stunts—two or more children
Wand Rowing
Chinese "Get Up"
Elbow Rock
Log Sawing
Camel Walk
Elephant Walk
Twister
Breast Stroke
Back Stretching
Wheel Barrow
(c) Acrobatics—individual
Head Stand
Cart Wheel
Front Roll
Back Roll
Front Roll to Back Roll
Back Roll to Front Roll
Broad Diver (two children)
Handstand
Hand Walk
(d) Acrobatics—two or more persons
Flopper (three children)
Twister
Belly Flip
Back Toss
Front Toss
Scrambled Eggs (three children)
Centipede (several)
Front Straddle and Back Straddle
Bobbin Back and Bobbin Front
Shoulder Stand (Partner hands)
Knee Balance from Crotch Lift

Handspring over Partner
Back Handspring over Partner
Shoulder Mount
Shoulder Mount from Back
Eskimo Roll

(e)   Relays
Tunnel Relay
Over and Under—2 balls
Staff Relay
Change Object Relay
Basketball Dribble Relay
Dribble and Short Relay

(f)   Group Games
Maze Tag
Do This (to rest)
Wand Jump—Relay
Jumping Circle
Spin and Hun
Last Couple Out
Black and White
Daddy
Railroad Train
Skin the Snake
Hindu Tag
Shuffleboard
Gym Soccer
Duck on a Rock
Broom Hockey

(g)   Contests
Wand Touch

SUBJECT MATTER
Physical-perceptual integration.

PROCEDURE
Games, which may be classified under two main headings: (a) quiet indoor games, and (b) active outdoor games. The indoor games are of special value when the weather is not suitable for outdoor playing. Many of the play experiences that are introduced in the physical education program may be used for the recreational pe-

riod. Too, the recreational games may be used or integrated with other activities.

D-7. *Snail*

OBJECTIVES
Same as **D-2, *Hop Scotch*.**

D-7. Snail.

MATERIALS

For this exercise a spiral whose outside diameter is about 7' is painted on the floor. The lines of the spiral are 8" apart.

SUBJECT MATTER

Same as **D-2,** *Hop Scotch.*

PROCEDURE

The child is shown how to "tight rope" on the line from the outside to the inside, heel to toe, without going off the line. Then he walks from the inside to the outside. The exercise is difficult and takes time for the child to master because there is a tendency to put both feet on the line side by side, instead of heel to toe.

D-8. *Spool Knitting*

OBJECTIVES

1. To develop advanced physical-perceptual coordination.
2. To develop the pupil's visual and kinesthetic sensations.
3. To provide opportunity for prolonged and intense concentration.

MATERIALS

Empty sewing thread spools, preferably the large spools, with four brads evenly spaced around the hole at one end, hereafter referred to as the "top;" cotton string or wrap, and a slender, rather sharp implement, such as a toothpick or needle.

SUBJECT MATTER

Manual dexterity.

PROCEDURE

Each child is provided with a spool, string, and the toothpick or similar tool. Drop the thread from the top through the hole in the spool, then hold the end of the thread at the bottom. Next, wind the thread around all four brads on the top, continuing past the first brad. Then using the toothpick, and holding the thread securely, take the lower thread on the first brad, lift it over the top thread and replace it on the brad. Continue this process for each brad.

After the child attains proficiency, different colors of thread may be used to make a patterned cord. These can be made into caps or other articles.

D-9. *Fabric Weaving*

OBJECTIVES

1. To develop physical-perceptual integration.
2. To develop "muscle memory," relating to tautness of the warp through hand, arm, and body adjustments.
3. To develop "perceptual memory" through memory for designs.
4. To develop the ability to concentrate on one activity while at the same time carrying on another.
5. To develop the ability to measure.
6. To acquaint pupils with various types of weaving.

D-9. Fabric Weaving.

MATERIALS

The *Comb Loom* which looks like a large "comb" is made from $\frac{1}{4}''$ white pine, 6" wide. (Another 9" wide loom is made from $\frac{1}{4}''$ oak.) Using a coping saw or a band saw, teeth are cut with the grain, and at intervals of $\frac{1}{4}''$. This leaves a series of slits, 4" in length, that separate narrow strips resembling the teeth of a comb. A reinforcing strip of thin oak $\frac{1}{2}''$ wide is glued to the top of the board, just above the slits, on both sides, and the same is done for the bottom.

This loom can now be cut into different widths; 2" being best for beginners. A hole is drilled in the center of each tooth of the comb with a small, sharpened finishing nail. In the case of oak, the holes are charred with a hot nail.

The *Harness Loom:* We use two looms of this type, one 30" wide, and the other 36" wide. The warp in each can be split to accommodate two workers on one loom. In this way cooperation can be learned along with measurements, colors, numbers, and proportion. Products of weaving are pillow covers, rugs, handbags, runners, scrapes and ponchos.

Definitions:

Warp—the thread which are extended lengthwise in the loom, and crossed by the woof.
Woof or Weft—these two words mean the same thing, i.e., the filling threads which cross the warp.
Web—a textile fabric coming from a loom.

SUBJECT MATTER

Manual dexterity, memory for design.

PROCEDURE

Comb Loom: To thread a 2" loom, measure warp threads twice the length of the web, plus 8". The first thread is threaded through the first hole and back again through the first slit. Another thread is measured and threaded through the second hole and back through the second slit. This is repeated until holes and slits are filled. Now, even all the ends and tie into one knot. Gather the loops at the opposite end, and tie, two at a time to a piece of dowel (a bit larger than a pencil) , 4″ log, spacing them to a parallel with the holes and slits in the comb. Tie a length of heavy cord around one end of this stick. To the knotted end of the warp threads tie a loop an inch or more in length. Place this loop over a nail or hooked screw fastened in wall or other solid place. Have child sit close to the end of the extended warp, pass the heavy cord behind him, and tie the loose end to the other end of the stick. This governs the tension which must be kept even at all times; leaning back tightens, moving forward loosens the tension.

By pulling down on the comb the warp in the holes goes down, while that in the slits goes to the top. This opens the warp shed so that the child can pass through it a weft or woof in the form of a narrow strip of soft cloth or a piece of cord. Raise the comb enough to make the warp threads even across, and pull comb toward the child. Then lift the comb, which will put the holes in the top position and the warp in the slits at the bottom, and the warp shed is again open to thread the weft through. Repeat the up and down movements of the comb, while "beating" towards the weaver's body at every change.

Patterns can be made by using several colors, such as checkers, stripes lengthwise or crosswise. The children are promoted to the *Harness Loom* when they are proficient on the comb loom. Here again, no shuttle is used.

Departure from traditional weaving:

The same soft narrow strips of "rags" are woven, but the ends of the strips are not sewed together. No bobbins or shuttles are used. The lengths of the strips are worked in the shed and overlapped end on end in much less time than it would take to stitch them together. There is constant finger work in this that is not to be had with shuttles, and the children can work at least five times faster. This is as far as our pupils usually go, but there have been those who have done well in camel harness weaving, Persian weaving and Turkish weaving.

General Remarks

Prolonged interest and concentration can be sustained in very few other activities. There are many issues which must be carried in the mind at the same time, such as correct tension, which color comes on the next shot, are holes up or down, counting of shots, measurement, even selvage, and listening to background conversation, etc.

D-10. *Basket Weaving*

OBJECTIVES
1. To develop fine manual dexterity and coordination.
2. To develop physical-perceptual integration.
3. To develop the ability to respond to and exercise tactile cues.
4. To develop the ability to create from a preconceived idea.
5. To create interest and skill in a hobby with vocational values.

MATERIALS
Round and flat reed of various widths and diameter; thin plywood; $\frac{1}{4}''$ and $\frac{3}{4}''$ pieces of solid wood, cut to shape for bottoms of baskets, trays, and other items. These are provided to avoid the necessity of weaving a bottom of reed, which is beyond the skill of our retarded children. Regularly spaced holes are drilled near edges of bottoms to hold heavier spokes, so the child can begin to weave in a very short time.

SUBJECT MATTER
Manual dexterity, spatial perception.

PROCEDURE
Long finishing nails are equally spaced around the edge of a small block to act as spokes that can't be pulled out of line. Pupil weaves a wet reed behind and before the odd number of nails as he continues around the circle. He is taught to use two, three, and four weavers, and is readily passed on to regular weaving where heavier spokes of reed are used instead of nails.

The wood for the bottom is shaped and marked by the teacher. The hole marks are made with a pencil holding compass which is set at the proper space. In most cases, the child drills the holes on the drill press.

When the child has achieved some craftmanship he is taught to use up to five weavers, to employ the arrowhead weave, to use Japanese weave, and to finish the articles by tying down the spokes into a braided top or bottom.

D-11. *Fling-a-Ring*

OBJECTIVES
1. To develop judgment of distance.
2. To develop physical-perceptual integration.
3. To develop a concept of positionality and directionality.
4. To provide an opportunity for individual and team competition.
5. To develop a sense of sportsmanship.
6. To provide an opportunity for integration in a group situation which stresses cooperation.

MATERIALS

Two upright poles, each 4' all and $1\frac{1}{2}''$ in diameter, made of wood or pipe. In each of the uprights there are four holes, spaced at intervals of 9'', starting 14'' above the base and ending 7'' below the top. Through each hole is inserted a length of round bar, $\frac{1}{2}''$ in diameter. These four round pieces protrude horizontally as follows: highest piece (close to top) 4'', next piece 5'', third piece 6'', and lowest piece $7\frac{1}{2}''$.

Four rings made of rubber or plastic hose, each $\frac{3}{8}''$ or $\frac{5}{8}''$ thick and with an inside diameter of $10\frac{1}{2}''$.

For Portable and Inside Use:
The base for each pole consists of either:
(a) A disc, 18'' in diameter, made of cast iron, $1\frac{1}{2}''$ thick, in the center of which is a threaded hole $1\frac{1}{2}''$ in diameter.
(b) A concrete disc, 18'' in diameter, tapering from 2'' thick at the outside edge of 4'' thick in the center, containing a T-pipe fitting, 6'' tall in center. A rope or chain is fixed on one pole and connected to the other pole by a snap hook.

For Fixed and Outside Use:
The base consists of a threaded pipe, $1\frac{1}{2}''$ in diameter and 6'' long, set in concrete so that the pipe opening is level with the ground.

D-11. Fling a Ring.

PROCEDURE

Position of posts:

(a) *Movable posts,* united with a chain or rope, are placed at agreed distances from each other (10′, 12′, or 15′).

(b) For *fixed* posts, threaded sockets can be placed in the floor or court so as to make the distance between posts 10′, 12′, and 15′.

The baffles of each upright shall point to the opposite post and be parallel to the tight connecting chain.

Each baffle shall be assigned a point value. Starting from top, and going down, these shall be 5, 2, 3, 5, and 10 for the base. A game shall consist of 100 points, or as many as agreed before the game starts. Tournament games shall be 100 points for adults at 15′, 50 for children at 10′ or 12′.

Flinging and Actions of Players:

The player, his foot either on the base or against his pole, throws the rings with the object of having them come to rest on the baffles of his opponent's pole.

Singles

The first flinger shall be determined by toss of coin.

The loser has choice of posts.

Each player shall have two successive flings to the post of his opponent.

At half game players shall change posts.

Doubles

First fling shall be determined by coin toss.

The winner shall have first and third flings, the loser second and fourth flings.

The flinging order, once started, shall prevail.

Each post shall be tended by a single player and one opponent.

They shall return the rings by flinging them in the order named above.

Partners may change post at half period.

Each player in both singles and doubles shall have the weight of one foot upon the base of his post from the moment of delivery until the ring has ceased forward motion. Failure in this shall result in the loss of any possible score and the counting of the fling. With fixed posts, the player must have one foot against his post. Penalty for failure in this, same as with movable posts.

Scoring

The score is totaled after the fourth fling. (In doubles, the scores

of partners are added together.) To score, a ring must stay upon
the baffle where it stopped.

The score for the fling is determined by the point value of the baffle
upon which the ring rests.

A ring that drops after once coming to rest shall be lowered to base
or removed from top before another fling. Such a ring has no value.

All rings resting upon a baffle shall score.

D-12. *Climbing Pole*

OBJECTIVES

1. To develop physical-perceptual integration through physical
exercise.
2. To aid the pupil to develop body control and postural adjustment.
3. To develop the ability to execute more refined motor tasks.
4. To aid the pupil to develop an inventory of bodily skills (involving the gross muscles) .
5. To aid the pupil to develop the concept of positionality
(height) .

MATERIALS

A 3″ steel pipe, 9′ high, set in a cement base. Around the pipe at
11″ intervals are rings of $\frac{3}{8}$″ garden hose, each ring held in place
by a slender stove bolt that pierces both hose and pipe. By tighten-
ing the screw, the bolt head as well as the smaller washer and nut,
which are also used, are safely indented in the hose ring. The ex-
cess length of bolt is cut away.

SUBJECT MATTER

Physical (motor) coordination.

PROCEDURE

Place child against and facing pole. He extends arms up to the
highest ring he can reach. With his hands behind pole and above
ring, he bends his knees. He thus must support his weight with his
hands. When he can do this repeatedly without fear, have him
draw up his knees, in preparation for climbing.

D-12. Climbing Pole.

From here it must be decided whether he will climb by locking his knees above a ring or by standing on a ring. If his choice is by holding with knees he may cross lower legs at the angles with the pole between his thighs. While legs are clinging to pole, the lower hand is moved on to a higher ring where the act is repeated. If he takes the second option, have him draw his feet above a ring and then lower them to standing position. As he straightens his legs he should go hand over hand above another ring. In either case the climbing distance of two rings should be sufficient for some time.

Add height slowly. Hold child against pole while learning. Be ready to catch child or break his fall if necessary, because many children stop climbing and let go for no apparent reason. They overcome this tendency.

D-13. *Junior Jai-Alai*

OBJECTIVES
1. To develop directionality and positionality.
2. To develop the ability to make quick decisions.
3. To develop integrated physical-perceptual skills.
4. To develop skills in group cooperation.

MATERIALS
Juice cans 7″ high and $4\frac{1}{8}$″ in diameter, open on one end, reinforced by $\frac{1}{4}$″ plywood discs at bottom, inside and out, fastened in place with a $\frac{1}{4}$″ stove bolt 6″ long. The bolt goes through a piece of pipe $\frac{3}{4}$″ in diameter and 5″ long, which extends out from the bottom of the can. The nut is on the inside and is kept tightened. A good grade of indoor ball 4″ in diameter or a rubber ball of same size that has been punctured and filled with yarn or light woolen rags. It must not have too much "bounce" to it.

SUBJECT MATTER
Physical-perceptual integration.

PROCEDURE
The teacher throws the ball toward the pupil, who tries to catch it in the can.
a. To catch:
   Show the child how to hold the handle with palm up, as a fencing foil is held. Stand 10′ away and toss the ball to the child so that it drops in an arc at the height of the child's eyes.
b. To throw:
   With the ball in the can, the knuckles of the hand in line of desired direction, the pupil draws his arm back, as in ordinary throwing, gives a pronounced whip of the wrist and stops the

movement quickly when his hand is in line with the target. Give practice at graduated distances in catching first and then in throwing.

Several well-known games can be adapted to the use of these materials. One wall handball is the first game that can readily be adapted to the can version.

To develop special skills, variations of soft ball can be played in which only the pitcher may handle the ball.

Volley ball can be played, the rules changed to balance the skill of the players.

D-14. *Carpet Chariot*

OBJECTIVES
1. To develop posture and balance.
2. To provide opportunity for group interaction and teamwork.
3. To develop sense of body adjustment to resistance.

D-14. Carpet Chariot.

MATERIALS

A strip of heavy carpet 28" to 30" wide and 54" long, folded double over a hardwood strip of wood 2" wide, $\frac{3}{4}$" thick and 36" long. Carpet is nailed to wood in several places with roofing nails and whip-stitched, with string, at end and selvages. A length of sash cord is tied to both ends of the wood strip. When pulled tight, it is 17" away from the center of the wood.

Another sash cord 28" long is doubled and tied to the middle of the short cord.

For hand holds, this long cord is tied in simple knots every 15". Another line is tied to both ends of the wood strip. It is long enough that a child hold it while standing upright on carpet.

SUBJECT MATTER

Balance, postural adjustment.

PROCEDURE

Each child should pull the empty chariot around the gym. The child should pull a fairly heavy load by himself to accustom himself to resistance and to the behavior of the load on a turn.

D-15. *Caterpillar (Tractor)*

OBJECTIVES

1. To develop positionality and directionality.
2. To further develop spatial sense and body orientation.
3. To develop physical-perceptual integration.
4. To develop sense of rhythm.

MATERIALS

A strip of snowfence, 8'6" long. It is made of twisted wire which acts as warp, and heavy lathes, $1\frac{1}{2}$" wide, which are woven 2" apart. These are cut to make a strip 21" across. The ends are brought together and wires are brazed to make a wide circle. The inside of the circle is covered with heavy carpet which in turn is covered with imitation leather or other waterproof material. The fabrics are held in place with upholsterer's tacks driven through both fabric and laths and clinched on the outside.

D-15. Caterpillar (Tractor).

SUBJECT MATTER

Physical (motor) coordination and rhythm.

PROCEDURE

The child gets into the caterpillar in a crawling position. From a position behind the pupil, the teacher grasps the edges of the caterpillar and slowly pushes it forward a short distance—two or three inches. After the child adjusts hand and knee position, repeat the procedure until the child can maneuver without help. See that there are no obstructions in his path. Make doubly sure he keeps both hands *inside* the circle at all times.

D-16. *Offset Tires*

OBJECTIVES

1. To develop physical-perceptual integration.
2. To develop directionality and positionality.

3. To provide opportunity for physically responding to rapidly changing conditions of balance.
4. To provide opportunity for decision making.

MATERIALS

Passenger car tire casings of various sizes. Cement weights (lumps of cement), varying in weight from three to five pounds, are fixed inside of the casings. The cement is held in place by two carriage bolts 3″ long, which pierce the tread and the cement and point toward the center of the circle. Two 3″ bolts near the ends of the cement lump are placed through the middle of the side wall. One unweighted tire casing.

SUBJECT MATTER

Balance, postural adjustment.

PROCEDURE

Teach the child to roll the regular (unweighted) tire first. Next teach him to roll a lightly loaded tire, keeping both hands on it at

D-16. Offset Tires.

all times. The next step is to teach him to roll it with a quick push of one hand while following it. When he can anticipate the erratic motions of the tire and respond accordingly, he may be promoted to the more heavily weighted ones. The tires are used in racing and in contests of distance and accuracy. In the latter instance, only one push is allowed from a given mark.

D-17. *Walking Maze*

OBJECTIVES
1. To introduce the pupil to simple problem solving.
2. To develop spatial awareness.
3. To develop positionality and directionality.
4. To provide opportunity for decision making .

MATERIALS
The maze is a rectangular paved area in which are set 54 four by four's, six rows of posts in width, nine in length. Each of these posts is grooved 1″ deep, from top to bottom on all four sides. There are, in addition, forty panels, 24″ wide and 42″ high which can be slipped into the grooves of the posts to form temporary walls, making possible an almost endless variety of pathways in the maze. The two long outside walls of the maze are permanent and 66″ high; the two short ends of the maze may be open or, if panels are placed in the posts, closed.

SUBJECT MATTER
Spatial orientation.

PROCEDURE
The child is first led into a simple maze which he can readily solve by himself. Gradually, by adjusting the panels, he is introduced to ever more complicated mazes, until he must really think to solve the problem.

At first, when the problems are relatively simple, the teacher remains outside of the maze but in plain sight at all times. Later, when the maze involves four or five turns, the teacher may stay in maze, but bow out of sight from time to time, constantly talking and encouraging the pupil in a cheerful tone.

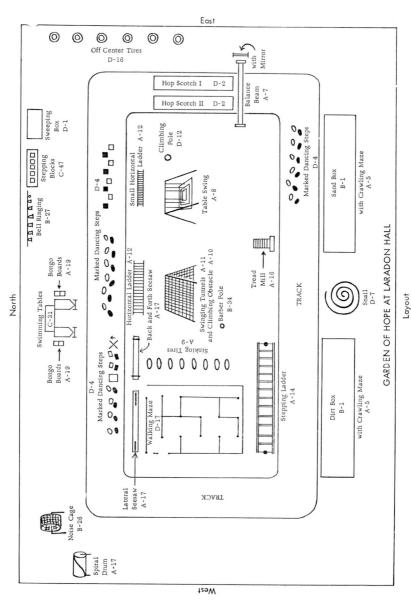

D-17. Walking Maze.

After three solo trips, four or more students may solve the problem simultaneous. Games of tag may be played in which *It* must be in the same lane as the one he tags. Older and taller pupils may work a regular sized pull wagon from the entrance to the exit at opposite end. This can be made more difficult in many ways, e.g., by making short turns or by lifting several panels just enough for the wagon to pass under, at the same time making it necessary for the pupil or pupils to go by a different path to find the front of the wagon before continuing the trip.

BIBLIOGRAPHY

1. Bancroft, Jessie H.: *Games for Playground, Homes, School and Gymnasium.* New York, Macmillan, 1937.
2. Baumgartner, Bernice B.: *A Curriculum Guide for Teachers of Trainable Mentally Handicapped Children.* Springfield, Illinois Department of Public Instruction, 1955.
3. ———: *Helping the Trainable Mentally Retarded Child.* New York, Teachers College, Columbia University, 1960.
4. Blodgett, Harriet E., and Warfield, Grace J.: *Understanding Mentally Retarded Children.* New York, Appleton-Century-Crofts, 1959.
5. Bradley, Betty H., Hundziak, Marcel and Patterson, Ruth M.: *Teaching Moderately and Severely Retarded Children.* Springfield, Thomas, 1971.
6. Descoeudres, Alice: *The Education of Mentally Defective Children.* Boston, Heath, 1928.
7. Doll, Edgar A.: Psychodynamics of the mentally retarded. *A.M.A. Arch. Neurol. Psychiat., 70:*121, 1953.
8. Doyle, Francis W., and Bower, Elizabeth M.: *Suggested Activities for Mentally Retarded Children.* Sacramento, California State Department of Education, 1952.
9. Dunn, Lloyd M. (Ed.): *Exceptional Children in the Schools.* New York, Holt, Rinehart & Winston, 1963.
10. Forel, August: *Hygiene of Nerves and Mind in Health and Disease.* London, John Murray, 1907.
11a. Frankel, Max G. and Smith, Maurice P.: Another approach to curriculum for educable and trainable mentally retarded children. Paper presented May 3, 1962 at Annual Meeting American Association on Mental Deficiency.
12. Frostig, Marianne: *The Frostig Program for the Development of Visual Perception.* Chicago, Follett Publishing, 1964.
13. Gellner, Lise: *A Neurophysiological Concept of Mental Retardation and Its Educational Implications.* Chicago, Illinois. The Dr. Julian D. Levinson Research Foundation for Mentally Retarded Children, 1959.
14. Goldstein, Herbert: *Report Number Two on Study Projects of Trainable Mentally Handicapped Children.* Springfield, Illinois, Superintendent of Public Instruction, January, 1956.
15. Guenther, R. J.: *Final Report of the Michigan Demonstration Research Project for the Severely Retarded.* Lansing, Michigan, State Department of Public Instruction, 1956.

16. Hafemeister, Norman R.: Development of a curriculum for the trainable child. *Amer. J. Ment. Defic.,* 55:494-501, 1951.

17a. Happ, F. William: Teaching Aids and Their Utilization for the Trainable Mentally Retarded Child. Paper Presented June 12, 1965 at Annual Meeting American Association on Mental Deficiency.

18. Hottel, J. V.: *An Evaluation of Tennessee's Day Class Program for Severely Mentally Retarded Children.* Nashville, George Peabody College for Teachers, 1958.

19. Hudson, Margaret: *An Exploration of Classroom Procedures for Teaching Trainable Mentally Retarded Children.* Washington, D. C., Council for Exceptional Children, 1960.

20. Itard, Marc Jean: *The Wild Boy of Aveyron.* New York, Appleton-Century-Crofts, 1962.

21. Jewell, A. M.: A follow-up study of 190 mentally deficient children excluded because of low mentality from the public schools of the District of Columbia. *Amer. J. Ment. Defic.,* 45:413-20, 1941.

22. Johnson, G. Orville, and Capobianco, Rudolph.: *Research Project on Severely Retarded Children.* Albany, New York, State Interdepartmental Health Resources Board, 1957.

23. Jordan, Thomas E.: *The Mentally Retarded,* 3rd ed. Columbus, Merrill, 1972.

24. Kephart, Newell C.: *The Slow Learner in the Classroom,* 2nd ed. Columbus, Merrill, 1971.

25. Kirk, Samuel A., and Johnson, G. Orville: *Educating the Retarded Child.* Boston, Houghton Mifflin, 1961.

26. Loos, F.M., and Tizard, Jack: The employment of adult imbeciles in a hospital workshop. *Amer. J. Ment. Defic.,* 59:395-403, January, 1955.

27. McCaw, Ralph: A curriculum for the severely mentally retarded. *Amer. J. Ment. Defic.,* 62:616-21, 1958.

28a. McGlone, Roy *et al: Aids for Teaching the Mentally Retarded* (Film). Boulder, Colorado, Thorne Films, Inc. 1964.

28b. ————, *Helpful Hints for Handicaps.* Denver, Colorado, Laradon Hall Publications, 1959.

28c. ————, *et al.: Teaching Aids for Mentally Retarded Children* (Catalog). Denver, Colorado, LADOCA Project and Publishing Co., 1. 51st Street and Lincoln.

28d. ————, *et al.: Functional Teaching of Numbers (Film).* Denver, LADOCA Project and Publishing Foundation, 1966.

28e. ———— *et al.:* Functional Teaching of Reading and Writing (Film). Denver, LADOCA Project and Publishing Foundation, 1968.

29. Montessori, Maria: *The Montessori Method.* Trans. by Anne E. George. New York, Stokes, 1912.

30. Mosso, Angelo: *Fatigue.* Trans. by Margaret and W. B. Drummond. New York, Putnam's, 1915.

31. O'Connor, N., and Tizard, Jack: *The Social Problems of Mental Deficiency.* New York, Pergamon Press, 1956.

32. Patterson, Ruth M. (Ed.): *Teaching Devices for Children with Impaired Learning.* Columbus State School, 1958.

33. Pearl, Norton H.: *Health by Stunts.* New York, Macmillan, 1919.

34. Perry, Natalie: *Teaching the Mentally Retarded Child.* New York, Columbia University, 1960.

35. Piaget, Jean, and Inhelder, Barbel: Diagnosis of mental operations and theory of the intelligence. *Amer. J. Ment. Defic., 51:*401-06, 1947.

36. Rosenblum, Marcus: *Unique Devices Teach Retarded. Rehab. Rec., 1:* 3-5, 1960.

37. Rosenzweig, Louis: Report of school program for trainable mentally retarded children. *Am J Ment Defic, 59:*181-205, 1954.

38. ———— and Long, Julia: *Understanding and Teaching the Dependent Retarded Child.* Darien, Educational Publishing Corp., 1960.

39. Sarason, Seymour B.: *Psychological Problems in Mental Deficiency,* 4th ed., New York, Harper, 1969.

40. ————, Davidson, Kenneth, and Blatt, Burton: *The Preparation of Teachers.* New York, John Wiley, 1962.

41. Seguin, Edoard: *Idiocy—Its Treatment by the Physiological Method.* New York, Columbia University Press, 1907.

42. Shaw, Lloyd: *Cowboy Dances.* Caldwell, Caxton, 1939.

43. ————, *The Round Dance Book.* Caldwell, Caxton, 1948.

44. Skinner, Burrhus F.: *Cumulative Record.* New York, Appleton-Century-Crofts, 1972.

45. Smith, Maurice P., and Means, John R.: Effects of type of stimulus pre-training or discrimination learning in mentally retarded. *Am J Ment Defic, 66:*259-65, 1961.

46. ————, *et al.: Guide for Functional Teaching of Mentally Retarded Children.* Washington, D.C., Report on research project RD-730, OVR, U.S. Dept. of Health, Education and Welfare, 1963 (unpublished report).

47. Standing, E. Mortimer: *Maria Montessori: Her Life and Work.* London, Hollis and Carter, 1957.

48. Stevens, Harvey A.: *A Curriculum for the Trainable Child.* Union Grove Southern Wisconsin Colony and Training School, 1953.

49. Strauss, Alfred A., and Kephart, Newell C.: *Psychopathology and Education of the Brain-Injured Child.* New York, Grune & Stratton, 1955.

50. Tudyman, Al: A realistic total program for the severely mentally retarded. *Am J Ment Defic, 59:*574-82, 1955.

51. Watson, John B.: *Psychology from the Standpoint of a Behaviorist.* Philadelphia, Lippincott, 1919.

52. Williams, Harold M.: *Education of the Severely Retarded Child: Class-room Programs.* U. S. Office of Education Bulletin, 1961, No. 20, Washington, D. C. Government Printing Office.
53. Wolinsky, Gloria F.: *A preliminary statement on perception in children —implications for instructional practices with retarded.* Paper presented May 8, 1964 at Annual Meeting American Association on Mental Deficiency.
54. Wolk, Shirley Mae: A survey of the literature on curriculum practices for the mentally retarded. *Am J Ment Defic, 62*:826-39, 1958.

APPENDIX

SECTION I

VALUES, DIMENSIONS AND COMPARISONS OF FUNCTIONAL TEACHING

Introduction

A MERE EXPOSITION of the devices or teaching aids employed in Functional Teaching may not readily reveal the values and dimensions of this program. Therefore, a discussion is offered here of the devices as they relate to the total teaching approach, in the hope that this may clarify and add to the descriptions of these devices in the context of teaching units which are to be found in Part II of the book.

They are elucidated here because they appear to be important, too important in fact to be left unemphasized and imbedded in Part II where more specific reference to the particular devices is made.

Value refers to the capacity of the device or maneuver to elicit for the user certain desired behaviors. These behaviors are seen in terms of their value in bringing about certain increments in learning. Dimension refers to the extent of these values—aspects which though not always readily recognizable, are yet significant. Comparisons are made to commercially available materials which, while appearing similar, often were conceived for other purposes. The comparisons are made to help elucidate the values and dimensions of the Functional Teaching materials.

A few devices have been chosen here as examples of what is meant. Too, if a teacher is to teach creatively and not mechanically, a wider understanding of the rationale underlying the devices utilized in this teaching approach seems mandatory. It constitutes an invitation to other conceptualists and practitioners to make changes and additions.

Dominoes With Pictures and/or Arabic Numbers (C-35)

On the dominoes used in Functional Teaching, the dots are replaced with Arabic numbers, pursuing the goal of teaching the child the *symbol and name of the numeral.* Thus the child learns to recognize numbers before he learns to count. Moreover, he learns to recognize and know the numbers in an easy, pleasant, painless way. He is not bothered at the start with value sequence; he learns first the symbol pattern of the number, then its name. Only after these two skills are acquired does he finally grasp the numbered sequence and value. Number recognition is emphatically stressed. To refresh the memory for numbers, to show a reason for numbers and to give a practical application of similarities and differences—these are some of the values of the Arabic Numeral Dominoes. They were developed in this particular manner in order that the children might see numerals in as many ways as possible.

Clock Dial (C-41)

The essential difference between ordinary toy clock dials and the one employed in Functional Teaching is that the latter not only has movable hands, but *detachable,* portable hands, held to the clock face by a suction cup. Thus the large (minute) hand of the clock can be removed while the child learns the hours in the one to twelve series. Later the small (hour) hand can be removed while the child learns the minutes in the one to sixty series. Eventually both hands of the dial can be used on the clock, thus enabling the child to master adequate time-telling. The clock is large and can be set on a table so the children can gather around it. Later, it can be hung on the wall as a regular clock for application of the learning.

Colored Nail Boards (C-17)

The Colored Nail Boards in Functional Teaching have definite and purposeful colored designs which help develop an awareness of both color and design. The series progresses from the simple to the more complex both in design and color. The number of nails used with each successive board also increases. The tops of the large-headed roofing nails are colored to match the colors on the peg board. Thus, color perception, similarities and differences may be brought out. Another value is ambidexterity (through inducing the pupil to use both hands) and, important, stress may be placed on speed of hand movement, of value for later vocational training.

The varied colored designs also offer great eye appeal which helps to prevent boredom with the task at hand.

Framed Inset Puzzles (C-1)

The puzzles used in Functional Teaching are of wood with only three or four pieces to each puzzle.

Commercial puzzles match by shape; an outstanding facet of the Framed Inset Puzzles is that they match both by shape and by color, but not simultaneously. Actually they are two puzzles in one. The child first fits the pieces of the puzzle according to picture or shape of the pieces—there is no color. The puzzle and pieces are then turned over and there is no picture. The pieces are now fitted by matching colors. The colors along the margin of the pieces are matched with the color along the margin of the puzzle frame.

Inset Puzzles (B-10)

The animal puzzles are designed so that each of the cut-out pieces are not cut at random; rather, they represent an indentifiable part of a particular animal. The parts are readily apparent. As an introduction, the child interlocks the pieces of the puzzle over a painted picture of the same animal. Later the picture is removed and the puzzle is assembled in a horizontal position (flat on desk) and finally, the puzzle may be assembled in a perpendicular (upright) position as explained below.

Mosaic Puzzles (B-18)

These Mosaic Puzzles are all symmetrical designs, with the purpose of teaching position, color, size, and shape. There are fifteen sets containing from six pieces to fifty pieces per set. The child starts with puzzle No. 1 and works through No. 15. The pattern for each puzzle is painted on an oil cloth and each piece of the puzzle has a different color on each side. Thus, if the child should put a blue triangle on the red of the same size and shape, he sees he is wrong, and must turn the triangle over to the red side. But just turning it over is not sufficient, as the triangle must be placed in the right position to fit over the pattern. This requires perception and decision-making on the part of the child which results from evaluation of his own work and correction of his own errors. The pieces are mainly angles, as angles fit together more easily than curved lines, and these are matching angles, all designed to increase the child's range of thinking. The child exercises visual perception and motor movement. When the child has mastered all the puzzles through Mosaic Puzzle No. 15, the same painted patterns (on oil cloth) can be hung on the wall and the child is instructed to make an identical pattern on the table in front of him. He must make the transition from a horizontal plane to a perpendicular plane. Such transitions offer quite a challenge to some children diagnosed as brain-injured, but it is one which they should be encouraged to accept.

Opaque Projector (C-25)

The opaque projector used in Functional Teaching is a commercial apparatus. But there is a specific technique for employing it. For example, it is not easy to teach safety to trainable children. By using the projector one can show a picture of a boy, a bus, a street and a sidewalk together and separately. Identification of each object is made, the questions are asked such as, "Where is the boy?" ("In the street") ; "Where should the boy be?" ("On the sidewalk"). The children *see* what is desired to be taught. The teacher can bring any message he wants to the children in a vivid, attractive manner.

An opaque projector is frequently used as an enriching experience, something in addition to unit lessons. In Functional Teaching it is used as a basis upon which to build certain concepts on understandings. For instance, it stimulates speech through discussion and comment; it is often the beginning of extemporaneous speech (particularly for the more nonverbal children) ; and it breeds some confidence, as the children are encouraged to speak in the dark!

Number Columns (C-40)

The *Number Columns* are designed as an aid for problem solution. For example, to add 1 plus 1 the pupil puts two rings on the units column, which would show "2" directly on the column. Thus, simultaneously, the student counts and sees what he is counting. When the child gets to 9 he sees there is no place for 10, so he must "carry over" by clearing the units column and starting on the tens column.

Number Columns provide visual, concrete action and transaction in introducing arithmetic, especially in the carrying-over in addition and the borrowing in subtraction; they provide a stable register of accomplishment even during the varying intervals of wandering thoughts or distractions so prevalent in developmental children.

Sentence Building Frame (C-21)

The device at Laradon Hall is what the name implies: a wooden frame with slots in which to slide words. It involves word matching. The child is given a "page" with sentences written out; additional duplicate words are set on the side of the frame. He is instructed to reproduce the sentences by arranging the duplicate words in proper sequence on the frame. This apparatus is designed to aid the child to develop proper reading habits, that is, to avoid skipping all over the page, to read from left to right, drop down to the next line and read from left to right, etc. The meaning of the words and the logical sequence of the words as parts of a sentence are pointed out continually by the teacher. Besides aiding in teaching the child to read in a proper sequence, the *Sentence Building Frame* helps build vocabulary and helps the child learn to express himself in complete and logical sentences.

Spelling Racks (C-27)

The Spelling Rack device consists of twenty-three sets or boxes of letters. The simplest set and its use may be described in the following example: The vowel and consonant EN is one unit. The letters T, B, P, D, M, H, are separate units. The combination EN is placed in the lower rack and the single letters in the upper rack. With EN and the addition of single letters brought down one at a time on the left, words such as ten, Ben, pen, den, men and hen are made. Phonetic consonant pairs are used and single letters can be brought down on the right side. Consonants which recur constantly are learned phonetically and by name. The child is never told that he is *making a word*.

The words are first built for visual recognition and pronunciation. Then one can branch off and words can be made by definition. As an example: "Make a word that is what we eat." The letters "OO" are already in the lower rack so the child brings down the "F" and "D." It is essential, eventually, to teach words by definition, because the child should know the meanings of the words he is using. The meanings of words are introduced slowly into the practice of making words. Ultimately the child is able to build words from functional definitions supplied by the teacher.

Word Matching Cards (C-19)

The cards used in Functional Teaching are small tabs with words painted on them. They are primarily used in word matching and recognition though the pupil is at first not burdened with learning the meaning or the definition. They are often used in a well-known game, generally called "Word Casino" (to bring in similarities and differences), along with the *Sentence Building Frame* (C-21).

Word Racks (C-20)

The rack is mounted, often on a fence out of doors. A mirror reflection is used to spot the letters of the particular word being spelled out as the students slide the letters into the rack. The apparatus fulfills a need for academic work with words (vocabulary building) with the added interest of the outdoors during pleasant weather. The letters are large so the whole class can participate at the same time.

Picture Word Book (C-18)

The *Word Matching Cards* (C-19) can also be used with the *Picture Word Book*. The pupil selects the tab that matches up with the word symbol which identifies the picture on the page. In this exercise there are three elements involved—the picture itself, the word symbol on the page, and the word symbol on the matching tab. There is a transition stage from the pure element of simple matching to a practical application, in the experimental sense, on the part of the child. Also the child learns to associate the word symbol with the picture and the sound of the word (similar to the objectives of the commercial cards).

Hidden Objects (B-17)

The objective is to develop sensory perceptiveness through organized play. As mentioned in previous chapters, a large part of the program of Functional Teaching is baised on the recognition of similarities and differences. *Hidden Objects* is designed to develop these perceptions (discriminations) *through* the sense of touch.

This device includes one box with a curtain and twelve additional boxes, each containing ten objectives. These provide the child with a great range of tactile experiences. The child puts his hand under the curtain and picks up an object; if he identifies the object correctly, he is allowed to take it out and place it on top of the box. The application is unique: in order to make for finer discriminaton and a higher degree of recall, the same object box is used at three different stages. The first time the child is allowed to judge by feeling the naked objects. The next time the objects are inserted into a bag of the thickness of a Turkish towel, and the third time into a bag of two thicknesses of Turkish towel. Each time a new problem is created, its solution leads towards refinements in modality learning through recall.

Tick-Tack-Toe (C-44)

The Tick-Tack-Toe game is the actual basis for the apparatus used in Functional Teaching. Large ointment cans, soldered shut and painted, are used rather than the usual X's and O's. We have found that the X's and O's tend to confuse the retarded child and that he is sometimes unable to draw them. There are two sets of grids for the game: one painted on a heavy tablecloth with other games; the other painted permanently on a table (the former can be rolled up and put away for easy storage and the table used for other things). The game is designed to improve attention and concentration and develop a capacity for plan strategy. It is designed to prepare the child for the future demands for socialization that will be made on him.

Sand and Dirt Boxes (B-1)

The distinguishing feature of the *Sand and Dirt Boxes* is that they are built high enough from the ground so that the children can stand while utilizing them. This feature permits the area beneath to be constructed as the Crawling Maze (A-5).

Weight Matching (B-11)

The *Weight Matching* idea leans heavily on Montessori (21) but as the meaning of "heavier than" and "lighter than" appeared too complicated for the developmental child at the outset, a set was devised wherein the weights are put into a sequence of light to heavy. Another set has four pairs of weights with very gross differences. A third set has weight-pairs with very fine differences.

Colored Cubes (B-14)

The main objective of *Colored Cubes* is to give experience in recognizing the different colors. By playing around with the cubes, the student comes to realize that he can change the colors by turning the blocks.

Discs on Nails (B-15)

Discs on Nails in Functional Teaching is a device requiring manual manipulation and coordination which utilizes visual and muscular coordination. The child matches discs with varying numbers of holes to bases with corresponding nail arrangements (they have one, two or three nails). The discs are to be placed on the nails so that they lie flush, one upon the other, and the child has to keep turning until the nails and holes match. Although the primary value is physical-perceptual coordination, at the same time the child learns colors, increases his capacity to attend, comes to realize the existence of similarities and differences, and to visualize spatial relationships.

Slot Boxes (B-3)

The *Slot Boxes* are boxes with openings of various sizes and shapes. Only a certain color block fits into each slot so the child must search for the one that fits. Each hole is exposed in turn. This brings out another unusual feature of the device. First, the child looks for a certain block to fit a certain hole, later he must reverse the process and look for a certain hole to fit a certain block.

When color discrimination is mastered the color blocks may be taken way and substituted with plain blocks to teach shape discrimination.

Fabric Weaving (D-9)

Weaving itself is almost as old as civilization. Looms of all types are offered for sale by various manufacturers for home and institutional use. Generally, the manufactured ones are hooked up so that the operator has only to lift the beam. This is not the case with the looms used in Functional Teaching. They are primitive type comb-looms with alternating holes and slots. Possibly the most unique feature is the special frame that permits retarded children to use these looms and do the weaving.

Pattern Column (C-4)

Most of similar commercial apparatuses consist of a series of graduated colored discs which form a cone when properly arranged on an upright dowel. The general trend appears to be to line up the discs according to graduated size, while the idea here is to line up the discs according to color or pattern. Also the discs turn easily and cannot come off. Another unique aspect of this column is the training of both hands in cooperation with visual cues. It is the development of this two-handed coordination that is one of the great values of the apparatus.

Shoe Lacing (B-25)

Shoe Lacing in Functional Teaching is a practical learning experience for the child, a step towards independence through self-help. The device is economical and durable. A shoe (sneaker) is imbedded in a cement and iron form. The weight makes the shoe heavy so that the child has a sturdy object with which to work. The child practices the lacing at chest level (on a table), at knee level (knee on chair with shoe in front) and finally at foot level.

It should be noted that this does not require the child to tie the shoe while it is on his foot. Such a task is too difficult if kept in context because of the complications it may introduce (need for support and balance, particular construction of shoe etc.,) during the learning period. In *Shoe Lacing* it is only after the main object is accomplished (skill in lacing and tieing) that the newly learned skill is applied in an actual shoe-tieing situation.

Bead Threading (B-6)

Many manufacturers put out beads and materials for threading of one sort or another. *Bead Threading* as used at Laradon Hall differs from these for the technique used is unique: The student threads beads by shape, color, and patterns from models he can see or according to verbal instructions from the teacher.

Dressing Techniques (B-24)

This can be compared to the Montessori dressing frames consisting of a snapping frame, zipper frame, show lacing frame, large button frame, and bow-tieing frame. They are simple processes isolated for practice and control of hand movement which is difficult for beginners. Cloth books are also obtainable which contain workable objects instead of words—items to button, snap and zip; shoes to lace and tie, etc.—all designed to entertain and train children to dress themselves.

Mr. McGlone's *Dressing Forms* are unique in that the child wears the form like a vest so that the buttoning or shaping procedure is not reversed as is the case with the commercial forms. The forms can also be turned upside down so that the buttons are properly oriented for boys as well as for girls. The child can practice while wearing the vest. Many retarded students are not able to see the relationship between a frame set on a table and piece worn by themselves. They may master the buttoning on a frame but cannot carry over the skill to manipulating the buttons on their own shirts. Caution should be expressed however, that too much stress on placing the exercise within the context of everday dressing can minimize the importance of accomplishing the main object (in this case skill in buttoning or snapping) .

Shell Puppets (C-16)

There are many types of puppets on the market, but none such as these. They are made from pecan, walnut, or other types of nut shells. The meat of the nut is removed and a face is painted on the shell. The heads alone made of nuts may be used, or they may be used with one piece costumes which can be devised. The whole class can participate with the help of the teacher. The apparatus offers a good incentive toward speech development in a nonstructured play situation.

Balance Beam With Mirror (A-7)

The *Balance Beam* at Laradon Hall differs from the many commercial ones by three major features. The beam has three interchangable faces (edges) twelve inches, four inches, and two inches wide. Each end is wide enough for the child to get a good start, thus he begins the maneuver with confidence. When the child has mastered walking the three faces of the beam, the beam is set so that the child walks toward a wall mirror. The student is told to watch himself in the mirror and to make his own decisions for body adjustment. He no longer will look down and watch his feet, but he can see them in the mirror. This requires a reliance upon perceptual-motor integration rather than upon more isolated perceptual and motor cues.

Climbing Obstacle (A-10)

Many companies offer similar contrivances in gym equipment.

In this device on one side the squares formed by the wiremesh are varied; they are larger toward the top and toward the bottom and get smaller toward the middle. The opposite side of the apparatus (the side the child climbs down) is made of very coarse wire mesh. The child first learns to climb up the coarse side and come down again. Later, as he acquires confidence, he learns to climb up the finer side, cross and go down the coarse side with a minimum amount of supervision.

SECTION II

EXAMPLE OF SEQUENTIAL LESSON PLAN FOR BASIC PERCEPTUAL DEVELOPMENT

Visual

I. Color
   A. Colored Yarn Board, B-9, pages 101-102.
   B. Bead Threading, B-6, pages 98-100.
      1. Thread large spools of the same color, for instance; red only, then green only, etc.
      2. Thread large beads, two colors alternating, then three colors alternating, and four colors alternating according to a given sample.
      3. Thread large and small beads alternating large-small with different colors of beads.
   C. Colored side of Versatile Sticks, B-35, pages 128-131.
   D. Use Jumping Peg Sticks for color identification, C-3, pages 134-135.

II. Shape
   A. Slot Box, B-3, pages 96-97.
   B. Stringing Frame, B-7, pages 98-100.
   C. Versatile Sticks, non-colored side, B-35, pages 128-131.
   D. Clear Stencil (circle, square, triangle, diamond) Catalog No. M137.
   E. Pattern Matching, C.8, pages 143-144.

III. Size
   A. Versatile Sticks, B-35, pages 128-131.
   B. Sorting in regard to size of various objects such as cups, balls, plates, etc.

IV. Color, Shape and Size
   A. Thread large and small beads alternating different colors, shapes and sizes according to a given sample.
   B. Versatile Sticks, B-35, pages 128-131. (using colored side).

C. Colored Nail Board, C-17, pages 152-153.
D. Pattern Column, C-4, pages 135-136.

V. Color, Shape, Size, and Position
   A. Pyramid Mosaic Puzzle, B-19, pages 112-114.
   B. Parquetry Inset Puzzle, Catalog No. W113.*
   C. Lacing Cards, Catalog No. P137.*

Auditory

I. Sound Matching, B-29, pages 123-125.
II. Bell Ringing, B-27, pages 121-122.
III. Masks and Bells, B-28, page 123.

Olfactory

Bottled Odors, B-2, pages 95-96.

Tactile

I. Hidden Object Box, B-17, pages 108-111 (boxes 1-3)
II. Feel and Match Texture Teaching Aids F5.**
III. Basic Shapes such as line, circle, square, triangle, made of sand paper mounted on cardboard.

Kinesthetic

I. Weight Matching, B-11, pages 103-104.
II. Nuts and Bolts, B-13, pages 104-106.

Basic Number Recognition

I. Number Identification, C-24, page 163.
II. Number Sequence Board, C-30, pages 173-176.
III. Counting Pan, C-33, pages 173-176.
IV. Dominoes with Arabic Numbers, C-35, pages 187-188.
V. Number Casino, C-36, pages 188-189.

Letter and Word Recognition

I. Alphabet Cards, Catalog No. 109.*
II. Picture Word Books, C-18, pages 153-159.

*DLM Developmental Learning Materials, 3805 Ashland Ave., Chicago, Illinois 60657.
**Teaching Aids, R.H. Stone Products, 18279 Livernois, Detroit, Michigan 48221.

Writing Readiness

I. Writing I, C-34-a, pages 186-187.
II. Writing II, C-32-b, pages 181-183.
III. Tracing of letters in the following sequence:
o/c/a/d/f/g/g/e/n/m/h/i/etc.
IV. Tracing of numbers in counting sequence:
1/2/3/4/5/6/7/8/9/10
V. Copying of letters in sequence
VI. Copying numbers

SECTION III

ADVANCED SUPPLEMENT TO C-40

Number Columns **(C-40a) (Page 192)**

Objectives:

1. To aid the child to note a step-by-step buildup of arithmetical understandings.
2. To aid the child, through concrete means, to comprehend abstract symbols and their application.
3. To develop initial number concept.
4. To aid the child to attend.

Subject Matter:

Perception of numbers for addition, subtraction, simple multiplication and division.

Procedure:

In the beginning of addition, subtraction, multiplication and division, the unit column is used *alone* until there is a strong feeling of confidence built in both pupil and teacher.

The pupil starts addition by using combinations through nine.

Problem: $2 + 5 =$

Solution: The pupil counts two counters aloud as he places them on the unit column. His attention is called to the fact that the column registers a 2 above the top counter.

From the box he places five counters on the platform as he counts aloud. He then places them on the unit column as he re-counts the 5. When in place the column will show the answer or sum 7.

To Carry Over a Number

When larger numbers are employed it will be necessary to use the other columns as the units grow into tens and the tens into hundreds.

251

Such a problem is shown to demonstrate the procedure of "carrying over":

Problem: $8 + 4 =$

or   8

$+4$
____

Solution: The pupil stacks counters on the unit column singly, and counts aloud until the column registers 8. He then counts out four more as he places them in a row on the platform. From this row the pupil fills the unit column as he counts "9." He then counts "10" when he places one counter on the tens column. It is very important that he immediately remove all of the counters from the unit column and place them in the box. There should, now, be one counter on the middle column showing "10." He then places the remaining two counters upon the unit column as he continues the count from 10, "11," "12."

By covering the 0 of the 10 with the eraser end of a pencil; he can be shown the number 1 that goes with the number 2 on the unit column that together make 12.

Subtraction

Subtraction differs from addition in that the involved numbers are set up on the columns at the start.

Problem: $8 - 2 =$

Solution: Place eight counters upon the unit column as they are counted aloud. Always see that the counted number agrees with proper number shown on the column. Remove two counters as they are counted, "1," "2." The answer 6 shows on the column.

To Borrow

Problem: $10 - 4 =$

Solution: Place one counter representing 10 units upon the tens column. Borrow one unit from this ten by removing this counter and placing it on end between the tens and hundreds columns. This will leave nine units which will be shown by placing nine counters upon the unit column. Take off four counters from unit column and put them in the box. The unit column will show 5. "Pay back" the one that was borrowed and left between tens and hundreds columns by placing it on the unit column. The column will show 6, the answer.

Multiplication

Problem: $3 \times 3 =$

Solution: Count one set of 3 counters on the platform. Put them on the unit column singly and place a mark where they stood. Repeat this procedure two more times until the number 9 is reached. Count the marks upon the platform which are three— shows that three sets of three each were placed upon the column to make 9. Or $3 \times 3 = 9$.

Division

Problem: $9 \div 3 =$

Solution: Place nine counters upon the unit column. Remove three of them and place them in a line across the board. Repeat this operation two more times. Count the rows of three to know how many threes there are in nine. (3)

Problem: $20 \div 5 =$

Solution: Place two counters upon the tens column to make it read 20. There is no counter on the unit column. A ten must be borrowed from the tens column to be later placed on the unit column. This is done by placing the number 20 counter on end to the left of and behind the hundreds column.

The unit column is then filled up from the box until it reads 9. A row of 5 counters is removed from the unit column and placed across the platform from left to right. A chalk mark should be placed on the front of the platform. Then take the remaining four counters from the unit column and place them across the platform parallel to the first row of counters. Then put the borrowed counter, which had been placed between the tens and hundreds columns, at the end of the second row. Make a second chalk mark. If there are enough markers (20) this action can be repeated to have four rows, of five each, across the platform. If counters are lacking, the first two rows of five should be placed in the box and the action repeated, using the number 10 marker on the tens column the same way as the number 20 marker was used the first time around. There should be four chalk marks on the front of the platform to indicate the four rows of five counters that are contained in twenty.

INDEXES

EXPLANATION

Each unit has:
(a) A stage letter indicating which of the four stages of teaching and training the unit is described under.
(b) A stage number after each stage letter indicating the place of a unit within each stage.

In order to make the location of a unit as convenient as possible, two indexes are provided:
(1) Alphabetical listing
(2) In the sequence of the instructional stages.

INDEX

UNITS, ALPHABETICAL LISTINGS

257

Name	Stage	Number
Pattern Matching with Optical Illusions	C	10
Pattern Matching (Automobile Cards)	C	13
Pattern Matching (Food Cards)	C	11
Pattern Matching (Photo Cards)	C	12
Photo Card Matching— see Pattern Matching (Photo Cards)		
Picture Word Book	C	18
Problem Boards— see Arithmetic Problem Boards		
Pyramid Mosaic Puzzles	B	19
Race Horses	C	2
Roller Skating	D	5
Sand and Dirt Boxes	B	1
Seesaws:	A	18
a. Back and Forth Seesaw		
b. Lateral Seesaw		
Sentence Building Frame	C	21
Separation of Objects A	B	4
Separation of Objects B	B	5
Shaded Yarns— see Colored Yarns (also Shaded)		
Shell Puppets	C	16
Shoe Lacing	B	25
Singing	C	26
Sinking Tires	A	9
Skull Pairing	B	16
Slot Boxes	B	3
Snail	D	7
Sound Matching	B	29
Spelling Racks	C	27
Spiral Drum	A	17

Name	Stage	Number
Spool Knitting	D	8
Stepping Blocks	C	47
Stepping Ladder	A	14
Story Telling	C	22
Stringing Frame ("Birthday Cake")	B	7
Suction Blocks (and Related Apparatus for Breath Control)	A	15
Sweeping Box	D	1
Swimming Tables	C	31
Swinging Tunnel	A	11
Table Shuffleboard	C	39
Table Swing	A	9
Thimble Box	A	13
Thinking Caps	C	43
Tick-Tack-Toe	C	44
Tone Counting	B	31
Treadmill	A	16
Treasure Hunt	B	32
Triple Card Matching	C	14
Value of Money	C	38
Versatile Sticks	B	35
Walking Maze	D	17
Water Pump	A	6
Weight Matching	B	11
Wired Hose	A	2
Word Matching Cards	C	19
Word Racks	C	20
Word Sequence Book	C	23
Word Development	C	29
Writing I (Exercises for "Writing Readiness")	C	32a
Writing II (Use of Pictures for "Writing Readiness")	C	32b
Writing III (Print Manuscript and Cursive Writing)	C	32c

INSTRUCTIONAL UNITS
STAGE A
BASIC PHYSICAL-PERCEPTUAL DEVELOPMENT

Name	Stage Number	Name	Stage Number
Feathers and Honey	1	Companion Cube	3
Wired Hose	2	Chasing Mirror Reflections	4

INSTRUCTIONAL UNITS
STAGE B
BASIC PHYSICAL-PERCEPTUAL SKILLS

INSTRUCTIONAL UNITS
STAGE C
ADVANCED PHYSICAL-PERCEPTUAL SKILLS

NAME	STAGE NUMBER	NAME	STAGE NUMBER
Pattern Matching (Photo cards)	12	"Writing Readiness")	32a
Pattern Matching (Automobile Cards)	13	Writing II (Use of Pictures for "Writing Readiness")	32b
Triple Card Matching	14	Writing III (Print Manuscript and Cursive Writing)	32c
Going to Town	15	Counting Pans	33
Shell Puppets	16	Ferris Wheel	34
Colored Nail Board	17	Dominoes with Pictures and/or	
Picture Word Book	18	Arabic Numbers	35
Word Matching Cards	19	Number Casino	36
Word Racks	20	Fantan	37
Sentence Building Frame	21	Value of Money	38
Story Telling	22	Table Shuffleboard	39
Word Sequence	23	Number Columns	40
Number Identification	24	Clock Dial	41
Opaque Projector	25	Number Book	42
Singing	26	Thinking Caps	43
Spelling Racks	27	Tick-Tack-Toe	44
Hoopla Ball	28	Manuscript and Cursive Writing	45
Word Development	29	Paper Beads	46
Number Sequence Board	30	Stepping Blocks	47
Swimming Tables	31		
Writing I (Exercises for			

INSTRUCTIONAL UNITS
STAGE D
INTEGRATED PHYSICAL-PERCEPTUAL SKILLS

Sweeping Box	1	Basket Weaving	10
Hop Scotch (and Related Games)	2	Fling-A-Ring	11
Bark Splitting	3	Climbing Pole	12
Folk Dancing	4	Junior Jai-Alai	13
Roller Skating	5	Carpet Chariot	14
Gymnasium Games	6	Caterpillar (Tractor)	15
Snail	7	Offset Tires	16
Spool Knitting	8	Walking Maze	17
Fabric Weaving	9		

INDEX

262   *Functional Teaching of the Mentally Retarded*

Index

Shaping behavior, *see* Successive approximations
Sheltered workshop, 48
Skinner, Burrus F., 17, 27
Social incompetence, 8
Stages(s), 70, 91, 131
Stamina, low, 8
Stanford-Binet, 59
Stimulation, sensory, 20
lack of, 30
Stimulus, 28, 34
Strauss, A. A. and Kephart, N. C., 28
Successive approximations, 27

T

Tactile sense, 37, 46
cues, 46
Functional Teaching devices, 37, 46
(in) perception, 43
Tasks for mental retardates, 10
Teaching
characteristics of MR children, 52-65
introduction to Functional Teaching, 12-16
objectives for Functional Teaching, principles and practices, 9-11
Tests
California Achievement, 62
Merrill Palmer, 57
Metropolitan Reading, 62
Peabody Picture Vocabulary, 58
Stanford-Binet, 59, 61
WAIS, 56-58, 59, 64
Thought process, 28
Trainable children
goals, 9
perceptual training, 13, 36-39

program, 14, 16
Trainable mentally retarded
characteristics, 7-8
curriculum guide, 9-11
educational goals, 9
follow-up studies, 52-65
research, 17-28
school program, 48-51

U

Units of experience, 24
Units of instruction, 70, 227

V

Values, 237
Vision, 31, 37
perceptual training, 36, 37
Functional Teaching devices, 37
Visual cues, 43
Visual perception, 30, 37
Vocabulary, letters, words and word combinations, 42
Vocational data, 54, 59, 60, 62, 63
Vocational training, occupational classes, 48-51

W

Watson, J. B., 30
Wild Boy of Aveyron,
background and behavior, 18
Itard, J. M., study and approach, 18
learning process, 18, 19
physical training, 20
Sequin study, 19, 20
sensory avenues, 19
Work experience program, 10
Workshop, sheltered, 48